While It Was Still Dark

It is one of my greatest joys to see women stepping out to follow their Savior, utilizing the gifts He has given them to encourage and edify the body of Christ, and Joelle is doing just that! As someone who has taught on Women of the Bible many times, it is so exciting for me to see Mary Magdalene brought to the forefront of our hearts and minds. Hers is a story I have loved, studied, and related to intimately and Joelle does a great job of connecting Mary's story to our own.

She has a fantastic way of writing that is easy to understand and relatable to us all. This book would be beneficial for both new and seasoned followers of Christ, and would be wonderful for individual or small group study. I love the Powerful call to action to be present in the life, death, and resurrection of our Savior! So needed! I encourage us all to press into that calling!

—**Ashley Possin**, Founder of *One Truth Ministries*, Speaker, & Bible Teacher.

***

'Beautifully disrupted' was I as I took in this thoughtfully written account of the life of Mary Magdalene & the ordinary, yet extraordinary way she followed Christ. *While It Was Still Dark* so wonderfully lays out the call to actively seek after Christ through His life, death & resurrection as a Christian woman today. Joelle, the author, captivated & drew me in as I read her candid stories, the humility she displays in her delivery, and her obvious understanding of God's word. I would highly recommend this book to any woman today looking for clarity, encouragement, edification, or simply a challenge to search deeper with Christ on how to lean into the difficulties of life trusting in God's greater plan. Five stars!

—Shelli Deniston.

***

While It Was Still Dark is a beautiful gospel-soaked read. Through a retelling of Jesus' life, death, and resurrection, I experienced newfound joy in the gospel and my call to follow Christ. Joelle traces the life of Mary Magdalene and other individuals from the Bible to show us what a life devoted to Christ should look like. I found myself convicted at many different points as Joelle discussed what it looks like to step out of my comfort zone and live-in joyful obedience and submission- a true challenge to our current cultural conceptions! Through both light- hearted and difficult personal stories, I found her to be honest about her own struggles while still calling fellow women to a bold faith. Joelle's heart clearly pours off of these pages. Her love for Jesus and desire for all to share that love is at the foundation of this book. It would be a treasure for anyone to read it!

—Grace Skelton, Pastors Wife and Stay-at-Home Momma of Four.

***

While It Was Still Dark is a beautiful picture of following Christ whole-heartedly. With careful attention to the details of Scripture, the author shows how Mary of Magdala devoted her life to being a disciple of Christ in His life, death, and resurrection, and how we, too, can embrace the call to love, follow, and serve the Savior. Using illustrations from Mary's life and honest, relatable stories from her own personal experience, the author brings to life a picture of choosing sacrifice for the sake of the gospel and the abundant life that follows a commitment to love and obey the Rescuer. This book is a must read, not only for those who have not met Christ and are looking for an honest and accurate representation of what a Christ-follower will experience and how the Lord will draw them closer to Himself, but also for seasoned believers who will find encouragement in the example of Mary's intentional dedication to her Savior, her pastoral care for those around her, and her joy in recounting the work of Christ. The author's bold yet gentle reminders of the beauty of the gospel and the hope we have of abundant joy in our dying to self were refreshing and life-giving to my spirit. If Mary was devoted to Christ in His life, death, and resurrection, then I can be as well.

—**Amy Herington**, Children's Ministry Coordinator, *Trinity Baptist Church, Jonesborough, TN.*

***

While It Was Still Dark wonderfully dives into Mary Magdalene's journey of faithfully following Christ through His life, death and resurrection. With Mary as her guide, Joelle explores what it looks like for a woman to wholly and completely devote herself to the Scripture and teaching of Jesus. From sacrificial obedience to welcoming suffering with joy, *While It Was Still Dark* is a loving reminder that our unwanted and unplanned "life disruptions" are most often what end up bringing God the greatest glory. Joelle uses her own life experiences paired with deep-rooted Scripture to lead the reader through difficult yet beautiful truths, all the while uncovering the ultimate gift of experiencing our faith to the fullest

—**Katie Keil.**
@katie.keil.

While It Was Still Dark

Joélle Davidhizar

While It Was Still Dark

Published by KHARIS PUBLISHING, imprint of KHARIS MEDIA LLC.

Copyright © 2021 Joélle Davidhizar

ISBN-13: **978-1-946277-92-3**
ISBN-10: 1-946277-92-4

Library of Congress Control Number: 2020952687

Headshot by Menhart Films and Photography.

All Scripture quotations, unless otherwise indicated, are taken from the Holy Bible, New International Version®, NIV®. Copyright ©1973, 1978, 1984, 2011 by Biblical, Inc.™ Used by permission.

All KHARIS PUBLISHING products are available at special quantity discounts for bulk purchase for sales promotions, premiums, fund-raising, and educational needs. For details, contact:

Kharis Media LLC
Tel: 1-479-599-8657
support@kharispublishing.com
www.kharispublishing.com

For Gran,

who believed in this book

before I did

TABLE OF CONTENTS

Introduction

So then, just as you received Christ Jesus as Lord, continue to live your lives in him, rooted and built up in him, strengthened in the faith as you were taught, and overflowing with thankfulness. Colossians 2:6-7

I once believed that before she met Jesus, Mary Magdalene was simply a prostitute. The story went something like this—poor, sinful Mary sat wallowing in her sexual sin on some dusty street corner before He brought conviction her way. This repentant harlot then followed Jesus, her rescuer, around for the rest of her life. As it turns out, Mary was not a prostitute after all.

Though we cannot be certain where the story started, somewhere throughout history we started merging the "sinner" in Luke 7:37 and Mary Magdalene.[1] So too, some link her hometown of Magdala with her character. The *Talmud* claims that Magdala was destroyed due to its sexual sin.[2] If Mary was a sinner, as Luke 7 claims, and her hometown was destroyed for harlotry, then she must have been a harlot—or so the logic goes.

While there is no biblical evidence to support this claim, the notion has lingered and many people still believe this today. Aside from the fact that she must have been a sinner because she was human, there is

---

[1] Herbert Lockyer, *All the Men/Women of the Bible Compilation SC* (Zondervan, 2005), 100

[2] Lockyer, *All the Men/Women of the Bible Compilation SC*, 100

nothing to suggest that her sin was anything more than yours or mine. Conversely, there is nothing to suggest that her sin was anything less than yours or mine either. While it's likely Jesus did not rescue her out of a life of sexual sin and torment, He did rescue her—and she would never be the same.

There is something about Mary of Magdala that has always drawn my attention. Maybe it's the fact that so many misunderstand her, or maybe it's the fact that she was one of the few women who lived among Jesus. Perhaps it has nothing to do with gender and everything to do with what she saw, what she felt, and what she experienced. Mary was there for it all. She walked with Jesus, ministered with Jesus, witnessed His death, mourned His loss, and ultimately, rejoiced over His resurrection. This woman encountered the Messiah in a way that makes me ponder, *What must it have been like to be her?* As my fascination with her story has grown, I have been struck by the few mentions of her in Scripture.[3] Though limited, her name occurs throughout the life of Jesus.

Three different times we find her presence in Scripture—in Christ's life, in Christ's death, and in Christ's resurrection—and I cannot help but wonder, isn't that where you should find me? Isn't that where you should find us all?

What does devotion to Jesus actually look like in a woman? Were you to randomly ask five women from your church this question, no doubt the answers would vary. To some, it might mean wearing cross necklaces and listening to Christian radio. To others, it could mean ensuring that you are at every church

---

[3] Matthew 27:56, 61; 28:1; Mark 15:40, 47; 16:1-19; Luke 8:2; 24:10; John 19:25; 20:1-18

gathering and say grace before each meal. Perhaps some might think it requires us to sell everything we own and move to a developing country. As a preteen, I was certain it had something to do with making sure my hemline was low enough and my neckline high enough (ah, adolescence). No matter where we live or how we've grown up, we all have a picture in our minds of what it means to be a follower of Jesus. Unfortunately, too often we're wrong.

This is where the account of Mary Magdalene's life can be of help. Her story is perfectly generic. We have very few solid facts about her life; scripture leaves the gritty details out, abandoning us to wonder. And yet, the generic nature of her story is what makes it so beautiful. That common woman, wholly committed to pursuing after Christ, could be anyone. Her story, devoid of specifics, could be your mother's, your sister's, your mail carrier's, mine...or yours.

Following Mary, as she followed Christ, can guide us in grasping the true nature of devotion. Devotion, though it looks differently for everyone, is at its very base the same for us all. Mary's life modeled this for us. Being rescued from much, she devoted her life to The Rescuer. She followed Him relentlessly—walking with Him through His life, His death, and His resurrection—and so can we.

Chapter 1

Present in His Life, We Welcome Disruption

My family and I host children through Safe Families for Children. If you're not familiar with the ministry, Safe Families for Children utilizes volunteers in the Church to care for children of families in crisis, while offering parents hope, healing, and restoration through intentional relationship. Essentially, it's a biblical model of hospitality that seeks to care for both the widow and the orphan.

While we consider this to be one of the most enriching parts of our life, opening our home to hurting children while opening our hearts to struggling families is far from easy. About a year and a half into our involvement with Safe Families, and just over a week into our eleventh placement, I found myself complaining to my husband.

"This is a total disruption of our normal, happy life." I felt the words fall out of my mouth and immediately caught them in my gut. *Yes, yes it is*, I thought. *But isn't that exactly what the gospel should be?*

There was never any doubt in my mind that we were being asked by the Lord to step into this ministry. I have a deep love for that little man that was living under our roof at the time, and I knew just how good and worthwhile that work was. And yet, there I was, complaining about the disruption of my own comfort. It's funny, isn't it? I beg the Lord to rid me of self, and then when He provides me opportunities to lay myself down, my first reaction is complaint.

We tend to build our lives like a tower of blocks. One block for family. One for friends. For our careers, education, dreams, hopes, fears, etc. We stack them up in nice little arrangements and right at the top, we place the gospel. It's neat. It's clean. It's tidy. And it's all wrong.

The gospel isn't meant to be just another block in the tower of our lives. The gospel is meant to be *the* block—the foundational block, the one on which we build everything. We cannot simply build our lives to our liking, taking our comfort into account, and then plop the gospel down on top like some sort of magical fairy dust. Too often we think that we can create our lives exactly how we want them, and God will smile on us. "Living my best life"—isn't that how the saying goes? We build and stack and then, almost as an afterthought, we add the gospel and expect our endeavors to be blessed. After all, we have a block for Jesus.

This is never how it was intended. The gospel cannot be our fairy dust, our last block, our afterthought. The gospel must be our foundation; we have to place it first. To do that, we must knock it all down; knock down everything that we stacked together so diligently, organizing and imagining what our towers will be when we are all finished. We guard and admire our self-made towers, and at the end, we call them "good." But Christ, in His wisdom and love, comes in and disrupts it all, every tiny block we've placed.

"You have no idea what 'good' is," He tells us. "Just you wait."

Disruption. Beautiful disruption.

Mary intimately understood this disruption. I would guess that she not only understood it, but savored it. Luke 8:2 tells us that Jesus released Mary from seven demons. There is some debate whether or not the number seven is literal or a symbol of complete oppression within her; but either way, it is clear that Mary was astonishingly tormented.

While Scripture does not overtly tell us what she experienced, the gospels give us enough information to draw a few conclusions. Firstly, Mary's oppression likely robbed her of any control she had over her body. In Matthew 17, we find a father bringing his demon-possessed son to Jesus. In this encounter, he expressed to Christ that his son often threw himself into fire or water.[4] Don't dismiss the gravity of that statement. The demons that oppressed this boy literally used his own body against him, torturing him with flame and sea. Not only that, but he regularly foamed at the mouth and gnashed his teeth. Matthew 9 recounts the story of a man who, once released from the demon that plagued him, regained his ability to speak. His oppression actually made him mute, thus his release returned to him his words. Conversely, Acts 16 tells us of a girl whose demon forced her to follow the apostles, calling out after them, making her a spectacle to all. Mary, we can conclude, was most assuredly enslaved in her own body.

---

[4] Matthew 17:14-21; Mark 9:14-29; Luke 9:37-42

Secondly, Mary's oppression likely robbed her of her dignity. The gospels' account of two Gadarene men possessed by demons gives us an idea of just how humiliating her plight might have been.[5] These two men had apparently abandoned their homes and chose instead to live in a graveyard. Not only that, but they did so nude. Scripture seems to point to this as a sign of their deliverance—that they were actually wearing clothes. These same men had been bound by shackles again and again, only to continually break free in fits of fierce strength. Homeless. Naked. Bound. Was Mary's experience similar?

Thirdly, Mary's oppression likely robbed her of hope. Imagine with me for a moment—a woman in Jesus' time without control over herself or her surroundings. Violent. Terrified. Perhaps she was homeless and nude, like the Gadarenes. Maybe mute like the unnamed man in Matthew 9. Maybe she was made to throw herself in fire or water time and time again. If seven demons truly is a metaphor for total oppression, it is not unreasonable to wonder if her experience was all of these things and more. Though we aren't told how long she was so oppressed, we do know that, had Christ not entered the scene, this would have continued to be her reality. Mary was suffering. Mary was trapped. Mary was hopeless.

But then, Jesus arrived.

Scripture does not tell us of this incredible encounter but we can imagine just how life changing this moment was for Mary. One moment, enslaved in darkness and fear. The next moment, free, face-to-face with the Messiah Himself. I often wonder how she reacted. Did

---

[5] Matthew 8:28-34; Mark 5:1-20; Luke 8:26-39

she laugh at the sheer outrageousness of it all? Did she dance, savoring her newfound liberty? Did she fall at His feet in gratitude, tears pooling in the dirt? Here was a woman completely without hope and then suddenly she was staring into the face of Hope Himself.

Disruption. Beautiful disruption.

Consider Joseph.[6] No doubt Joseph's life was going as expected, perhaps even better than expected, when we begin the account of his life in Genesis. Joseph was the favored son of Jacob. After receiving two dreams from God, he was confident that someday his brothers, who currently despised him, would bow down to him. All was going according to plan until the day those same brothers faked his death and sold Joseph into slavery.

Disruption.

Joseph eventually found favor with Potiphar, the captain of Pharaoh's guards, and was given a job in his house. He was so well respected that Potiphar entrusted all that he owned to Joseph. You can imagine Joseph's relief as things began to go well for him again; from lowly slave to honored servant. But then, Potiphar's wife falsely accused Joseph of attempting to take advantage of her, resulting in her enraged husband banishing Joseph to prison.

Disruption. Again.

Can you feel the disappointment and sense of futility Joseph must have experienced? The weight of hopelessness he must have carried? Betrayed and discarded, yet again. Did he break down in tears as the

---

[6] Genesis 37; 39-50

prison doors closed? Did he yell at the ceiling or beat his hands against the wall? Did he quietly resign himself to a life of suffering and struggle? Did he start to question whether or not God could truly be good, or worse yet, if He existed at all?

Fortunately, this is not the end of Joseph's story. At last, he finds favor with Pharaoh himself and is given authority over all of Egypt. This position would allow him to help the nation of Egypt in a time of great need, and would lead to a beautiful reunion between he, his brothers, and his father.

Take note—the disruptions in his life became the very thing that God used to bring about His glory. Looking back on the years since being sold into slavery, Joseph would tell his brothers, "God sent me ahead of you to establish you as a remnant within the land and to keep you alive by a great deliverance. Therefore, it was not you who sent me here, but God."[7] Talk about a godly perspective! In his wisdom, Joseph was able to see that the disruptions in his life, that were so devastating at the time, could only be the hand of God, working out His ultimate plan.

Consider Esther. Esther was a Jewish girl whose parents had died, leaving her in the care of her cousin. We don't know much more when Scripture picks up her story, but anything more is unnecessary. We can assume this young girl was living a very ordinary life when suddenly she is swept up and taken to live in the king's palace. No choice. No say. No way out.

---

[7] Gen. 45:7-8a

Disruption.

At the urging of her cousin, she conceals her heritage from the king. For twelve months she is forced to endure extensive beauty treatments before Esther ultimately finds favor with the king and becomes queen. Just as with Joseph, this position would prove to be critical to accomplishing the ultimate plan of God. As queen, Esther would save the Jewish nation from genocide, rescuing God's chosen people.

Disruption. Beautiful disruption.

Women who choose to be present in the life of Christ will experience disruption. There will surely be moments, like Mary's, in which we are moved from darkness to light, from hopelessness to hope, from death to life itself. Those moments will cause us to laugh, and dance, and cry tears of joy. "I once was bound but now I'm free," we'll shout. "Christ has brought disruption for me!"

But there will also be moments like Joseph's, when everything seems to be falling apart. We will have moments like Esther's, in which everything that we had known is quickly lost, and there will assuredly be many little moments like mine, in which we are moved out of our comfort and into the uncomfortable work of the gospel. It's altogether simple to rejoice with Mary in those times of disruption that lead us to light, and yet, the Father deserves our praise all the more for the disruptions that seemingly lead us into the darkness as we follow hard after Him. If following Christ requires us to take up our cross, then disruptions will come. Isaiah 55:8-9 says,

For my thoughts are not your thoughts,
neither are your ways my ways, declares the Lord.

For as the heavens are higher than the earth,
So are my ways higher than your ways
And my thoughts than your thoughts.

Had Joseph been given the option, it is unlikely he would have chosen to be sold into slavery, falsely accused, and thrown into prison. Esther would surely have chosen a different path for her life, but God's ways are not our ways.

Imagine you were given a giant box of dominos and were instructed to create a train. This train would need to be constructed so that when the first domino was knocked over, it would begin a chain reaction that would result in the fall of the last domino. Now, imagine you aren't given the last domino, but are simply told it exists and your train has to knock it over—it's your job to set the dominos up the correct way, and you only get one chance. Not only that, but the last domino is hidden one hundred yards away, through the woods, in the dark, and you aren't given a light. It would be near impossible for you to complete that task!

Let's take it one step further. Imagine you were told to create the train using all the dominos, but were not even informed that there was a hidden last domino, lurking in the dark woods. Would your train knock it down? Of course, it wouldn't! You didn't know you had a goal to reach! You didn't have all the information to work it out perfectly! You, in your limited understanding, couldn't see the big picture.

This is why we can rejoice when disruptions come. God has the unique ability to hold the past, present, and future in His hands and chooses the perfect path for our lives to take for His glory. He's omniscient—

all-knowing—He sees all the dominos and knows just where to place the next to get us to the end. God's plans for our lives often involve trial and heartbreak, sorrow and confusion, but God's plans are better. How wonderful is that truth! Christ will lovingly tear down the block towers of comfort that we have built for ourselves and in their place He will give us His very Self. "He is working out His perfect plan," we'll shout. "How gracious He is to bring disruption for me!"

***

Our first house was a sweet 1940s three bedrooms in a historic part of our city. We fell in love with the tiny front porch just big enough to fit a small bench and a chair, the elementary school across the street complete with three playgrounds, and how close it was to movie theaters, grocery stores, parks, and pools. I was pregnant with our second when we moved in, one incredibly snowy day in January. As I fell asleep that night on the floor of our new living room, snoring toddler curled up next to me, I remember quietly praising God for the gift of that place.

It wasn't long before we settled into that house and neighborhood. We found our rhythm in long walks to bookstores and coffee shops, and took frequent advantage of the playgrounds across the street. As the years passed, however, we came to understand that as much as the proximity to everything was a blessing, it came with some disadvantages. Proximity meant foot traffic and foot traffic often meant trouble. It started out small, boots stolen off our porch and cars rifled through during the night. We prayed, started double-checking locks, and resigned ourselves to this one minor inconvenience. Things would happen occasionally but we never felt fearful or anxious. God had brought us to that place and that was enough.

Then one night, my husband and I woke to our dog barking fiercely. Entering the living room, we found our German Shepherd mix attacking the front door— the handle wiggling. Someone was trying to get into our home and neither our presence nor our dog's barking was deterring him. My husband dialed 911 and planted himself in front of the door. I rushed to our children's rooms as our would-be intruder attempted to open window after window. Surprisingly, all four children were sleeping peacefully, completely undisturbed by the commotion around them. While we waited for the police to arrive, I sat on their beds and prayed protection over each of them, asking the Lord to guard them and keep them. Fortunately, the police arrived quickly, their lights scaring off the nighttime visitor before they had gotten to our drive. The officers took a description, chased after him, and that was that.

After the police had gone and the dog had stilled, my husband and I sat up marveling at God's provision, specifically over our children. Contrary to everything around us, our home had been characterized by peace that night. Both of us had been able to think clearly and calmly as we attempted to deal with the uninvited guest and all four of the children in our home did not so much as stir throughout the ordeal. This was nothing short of a miracle. On any given night, we couldn't so much as watch a movie in the living room without waking at least one of our kids. Our home was small and the kids' rooms were at the front of the house. Usually, a belly laugh or a door closing would wake the whole troop, and yet, there they were, sleeping soundly through a dog barking, phone conversations with dispatchers, police officers walking the perimeter, my constant walking in and out of their rooms praying, and a man actively trying to get into their home. Nothing, not one thing, disturbed their sleep.

As I sat in the dark, watching them sleep, Psalm 23 filled my mind.

> *The Lord is my shepherd; I shall not want.*
> *He makes me lie down in green pastures.*
> *He leads me beside still waters.*
> *He restores my soul.*
> *He leads me in paths of righteousness*
> *For His name's sake.*
> *Even though I walk through the valley of the shadow of death,*
> *I will fear no evil,*
> *For you are with me;*
> *Your rod and your staff, they comfort me.*
> *You prepare a table before me in the presence of my enemies;*
> *You anoint my head with oil;*
> *My cup overflows.*
> *Surely goodness and mercy shall follow me all the days of my life,*
> *And I shall dwell in the house of the Lord forever.*

Is it any wonder this psalm is so well-loved? The picture of peace and the truth found in these verses is enough to make even the most trying of situations seem a bit more bearable. Those four children on that chaotic night were a perfect picture of Psalm 23 peace. When all was uncertain around them, they remained unshaken. When trouble abounded, they were undisturbed. When an enemy lurked at their door, they kept at rest.

This is the kind of peace offered to us even as we face the scariest unknowns. My children went to sleep that night completely assured that my husband and I were watching over them. They didn't have to worry about the things that go bump in the night—their parents were with them.

When the disruptions in your life bring uncertainty, do you carry Psalm 23 peace, trusting in the care of the Good Shepherd, or do you find yourself overcome with anxiety and fear? Are you able to rest in the midst of trial, taking hold of the meal God has offered you, or are you too panicked to even notice the table? Joseph and Esther were certainly given opportunity to succumb to fear and yet their lives were marked by submission to the will of God and an unwavering hope. Esther was so convinced of God's goodness and so determined to do what was right that she, when faced with the very real possibility of death, announced confidently that, "if I perish, I perish." Peace, disruption, confidence, uncertainty, all walking hand-in-hand. This is what is offered to the believer. As my children could rest without fear knowing that their parents were there, so we can rest without fear knowing Who is with us. Yes, disruptions will come. Yes, enemies will threaten. Yes, the valleys will be dark and the nights too long, but in them we will find a table—and He will be with us.

Go Deeper:

1. Recall a time that God brought disruption into your life. How have you seen God's faithfulness in that?

2. When your plans get off track, what is your first reaction? Submission? Fear? Anxiety? Peace? What can you do to ensure you keep a godly mindset when disruptions come your way?

3. Read the book of Ruth. When faced with disruption, is your attitude more like Naomi's or Ruth's?

4. Read Psalm 23. Write out your favorite verse from the chapter and thank God for making His peace so readily available to us.

Chapter 2

Present in Christ's Life, We Sacrifice

When my oldest son was in preschool, I had Proverbs 31:10-31 written out and hanging on my refrigerator. It's a challenging passage—a picture of the kind of woman I so desire to be. When we had just started hosting children, I often found myself overwhelmed, stretched thin, and at my breaking point in front of that fridge reading those verses. It wasn't even 6:15 one morning before I was doing exactly that, clinging to the description of that woman. "Lord, let me be like her," I prayed. Read it with me.

Who can find a wife of noble character?
She is far more precious than jewels.
The heart of her husband trusts in her,
And he will not lack anything good.
She rewards him with good, not evil,
All the days of her life.
She selects wool and flax
And works with willing hands.
She is like the merchant ships,
Bringing her food from far away.
She rises while it is still night
And provides food for her household
And portions for her female servants.
She evaluates a field and buys it;
She plants a vineyard with her earnings.
She draws on her strength

And reveals that her arms are strong.
She sees that her profits are good,
And her lamp never goes out at night.
She extends her hands to the spinning staff,
And her hands hold the spindle.
Her hands reach out to the poor,
And she extends her hands to the needy.
She is not afraid for her household when it snows,
For all in her household are doubly clothed.
She makes her own bed coverings;
Her clothing is fine linen and purple.
Her husband is known at the city gates,
Where he sits among the elders of the land.
She makes and sells linen garments;
She delivers belts to the merchants.
Strength and honor are her clothing,
And she can laugh at the time to come.
Her mouth speaks wisdom,
And loving instruction is on her tongue.
She watches over the activities of her household
And is never idle.
Her children rise up and call her blessed;
Her husband also praises her;
"Many women have done noble deeds,
but you surpass them all!"
Charm is deceptive and beauty is fleeting,
But a woman who fears the Lord will be praised.
Give her the reward of her labor
And let her works praise her at the city gates.

What a passage. What a woman. As is so often the case, a part of that passage struck me anew and flooded me with conviction that morning. "She opens her hand to the poor and reaches out her hands to the needy."

You see, the previous day we had been called about a new child that needed caring for and had committed to pray over him for the night. With three small children, adding even one more child to our crew was a big undertaking. It's not as easy as simply putting another car seat in the minivan. Opening our home to extra children also means adjusting our family to a new dynamic—a dynamic that often comes with abundant tears (mine) and too many sleepless nights (also mine). I woke up after that night of prayer too early with too little energy and too much self-pity. I kept thinking, "I am too tired/overwhelmed/busy to take another child right now." But then, the fridge.

That word "reaches" weighed on me so heavily that I finally read through every occurrence of it in Scripture, and do you know what I found? It always carries with it a sense of something stretching itself out and a couple times literally translates as "touches." Wow.

Put another way, Proverbs 31:20 could read, "She opens her hand to the poor and stretches out to touch the needy."

This is not passive. This is intentional and requires action, but this is good. I was tired; I was just so tired, but in my "tired" was I willing to reach out to the hurting around me?

While discussing the potential placement with my children, my son expressed hesitation before my oldest softly said, "We have a bed for him."

Isn't it that simple? Or rather, shouldn't it be that simple? My then four-year-old pointed out the reality of what we were facing. A little boy needed something we had readily available. How could we possibly turn him away?

Unfortunately, everything human in us rebels against these potentially simple sacrifices. We want to be sacrificial. We want to serve those around us. We want to emulate the Proverbs 31 woman. And yet, we struggle to find the means to do so.

Ever since the Fall we have been bound by these earthly bodies. They are not invincible. They do not have everlasting energy. They push against us daily. Our bodies themselves weigh us down; and our minds, so easily manipulated, trick us into following our flesh rather than our Father. So often we find ourselves resonating with the Apostle Paul:

> *For I know that nothing good lives in me,*
> *that is, in my flesh.*
> *For the desire to do what is good is with me,*
> *but there is no ability to do it.*
> *For I do not do the good that I want to do,*
> *but I practice the evil that I do not want to do.*
> (Romans 7:18-19 CSB)

Paul's lament is our own. We don't have to imagine what this must have been like for him. We understand this intimately because we see this pattern play out in our lives time and time again. The church's nursery needs volunteers, but sacrificing that hour each week is just too much. You see an elderly neighbor struggling to pull out her garbage bins and think, *I should really help with that next week*, but when next week rolls around you put it off to "next week" again. Maybe you see the caller I.D. of a particularly needy friend and think to yourself, *I just can't deal with that right now*, while letting it go to voicemail.

You're guilty of it. I'm guilty of it. We're all guilty of it. We see a need and decide that we don't have the energy to deal with it just then, or really ever. We let our busy schedules and tired bodies deceive us into believing that we lack what we need to serve right this moment, but the Bible tells us a different story. Ephesians 2:10 reads,

> *For we are his workmanship,*
> *created in Christ Jesus for good works*
> *which God prepared beforehand,*
> *that we should walk in them.*

Paul asserts that believers have been set aside for specific good works that were prepared for us ahead of time. Since we know that "all things work together for good for those who are called according to His purpose," [8] we can assume that these works were perfectly and intentionally chosen for us—individually as well as corporately. How freeing that is! The God who knows your every weakness and strength, every fear and desire, handpicked the ways you get to serve in the body of Christ. If this is indeed true, we must already be equipped for these acts of service and sacrifice. God didn't miscalculate when He sent that neighbor your way. He didn't accidentally type out your phone number when He meant to dial Brenda's. He is completely and totally incapable of making a mistake. The need that coincidentally fell into your lap is most likely no coincidence at all. That opportunity to serve was meant for you, right now, and if that's so, you must have everything you need to walk in it, right now.

2 Peter 1:3 puts it this way,

---

[8] Romans 8:28

His divine power has given us everything required
for life and godliness through the knowledge of him
who called us by his own glory and goodness.(CSB)

Now, I am not arguing that we are required to take every opportunity to serve that comes our way. No. There are far too many opportunities and far too little time to honor both God and our families well with that mindset. I am, however, arguing that we too often wait until we are less tired, less busy, less stressed or overwhelmed, to start serving, when in fact God has laid out good works for us to do right this second. These works are not contingent on how we feel in the moment or what our schedules look like, but rather on what we have been given already—everything required for life and godliness. We need only look to the life of Jesus to see.

And rising very early in the morning,
while it was still dark,
he departed and went out to a desolate place,
and there he prayed.
Mark 1:35

As much as we've experienced exhaustion, I imagine Jesus experienced much more. Before this particular early morning, Jesus had spent His previous day preaching the Good News, casting out demons, and healing many. Mark 1:32-34 tells us that once the sun had set, after the Sabbath had ended, "the whole city was gathered together" at the door where Jesus was, waiting for Him to heal them. Though most likely not every citizen was in attendance, it is clear that a large crowd had followed Jesus, anticipating Him working on their behalf. Work He did, healing and casting out demons, we can assume, well into the night.

You've had long nights. I have too. Usually, the last thing we want to do after a night like that is wake up early. "I deserve a little extra sleep," we tell ourselves. "After all, I was up so late." No doubt Jesus felt the tug of his bed and the weight of his tired body that morning, and yet He didn't let the pillow pull him back to sleep. He didn't justify a slow morning of recuperation. He got up "very early" and spent time with the Father in prayer.

Many of us prioritize time in the morning for prayer and the Word. Some of us find the time while our kids nap or on our lunch break. Still, others desire to spend that time with God but have never been able to get into a consistent routine. Life just seems to get in the way. It happens. I've been there. Whether I was waking constantly to feed and soothe infants or staying up too late writing papers, exploring cities, and talking with friends, I have de-prioritized my time in the Word throughout different seasons of my life. I told myself that it was okay—that I could still follow after God without seeking Him in the Word and everything would turn out fine. I lied to myself, and each time I suffered for it. 2 Timothy 3:16-17 says,

> *All Scripture is breathed out by God*
> *and profitable for teaching,*
> *for reproof, for correction,*
> *and for training in righteousness,*
> *that the man of God may be competent,*
> *equipped for every good work.*

That time Jesus spent with the Father that dark morning was not just some passing fancy, a fleeting desire He fulfilled and moved on from. No, it was essential. It was important. It was necessary. It equipped Him to do what He needed to do next. That very day,

Jesus would continue on to the neighboring cities to preach the gospel. "This is why I have come,"[9] He said. Just like us, Jesus had good works set out before Him. He understood this, He accepted it, and He chose to prioritize that which would equip Him to walk in them.

The Bible is not simply a book of history, stories, or a list of to-dos. The Bible is the very Word of God. Its words bring us comfort in times of mourning, encourage us with accounts of God's past provision and promises of future hope, and challenge us to better represent Christ to those around us. This is the main way God speaks to us and, as Paul writes, is what makes us competent and equipped for every good work.

As women, we will never be able to walk in the good works that have been set before us if we do not prioritize time in prayer and the Word. Jesus Himself, God incarnate, sacrificed sleep so that He might be equipped to sacrifice later. So too we must sacrifice for the first thing of seeking the face of God if we are to be able to sacrifice for the second—our families, our churches, our neighbors. Too often we choose to skip our time in Scripture and prayer so that we can get x, y, or z done. Is it any wonder that when those opportunities to walk in good works arrive, we "just don't have the energy right now?" We've given up the very thing meant to equip us!

When faced with the opportunity to serve that family and that little boy all those years ago, my flesh rebelled. My body was tired and my mind weary, but I lacked nothing. I had no desire to extend my hands to the poor and the needy, but I had everything necessary

---

[9] Mark 1:38

to do so. That hosting I so dreaded ended up bringing me joy and laughter. Looking back, that was the placement that caused me to fall in love with the work God was asking us to do. I would have missed it had I followed my fleshly fear rather than my faithful Father.

After being freed from demonic oppression, Mary could have easily thanked Jesus and run off to her hometown. No doubt she had parents, siblings, and friends who would have rejoiced to see her healthy and in her right mind again. It would have been logical for her to return home and spend the rest of her days with her family, but this is not what Mary did. Mary chose a different way. Mary recognized that the Messiah was worth following and chose to sacrifice whatever lay behind her in favor of time with Christ. Wherever He went, she went. Not only that, Mary would go on to support Jesus' earthly ministry financially as well. Had she returned to Magdala, she would have never been able to walk in that good work—the work He had planned for her. Her sacrifice of her previous life as she sought to know Jesus would enable her to further sacrifice towards the work of the gospel.

So too our lives as women wholly devoted to Christ should be marked by sacrifice. John 15:13 says,

> *Greater love has no one than this,*
> *That someone lay down his life for his friends.*

We often relate this verse solely to physical death. While yes, it absolutely carries that sense, limiting the meaning to physical death alone does not grasp the fullness of the text. Laying down our lives means so much more than being willing to die for someone. It means offering up our free time. It means opening up our spare bedroom. It means giving away our money. It means pouring out our energy. It means sacrificing our rest. Following Christ in His life means offering up our very selves for those around us, but we cannot do it without that equipping time in prayer and the Word. Are we laying down our lives daily for the first thing of seeking the Lord? Only then will we be able to lay down our lives for the second things, and all the rest to come.

Go Deeper:

1. Do you set aside time each day for prayer and Bible reading? If not, what's standing in your way?

2. When opportunities to serve come your way, do you find yourself reacting with joyful submission or with self-centered grumbling?

3. Take an inventory of your day. Ask the Lord to reveal to you what things you need to lay down in order to make time for Him in the word and in service.

Chapter 3

Present in Christ Life, We Follow…then Lead

Have you ever tried to walk through deep snow? Having grown up in the Silicon Valley, this was a foreign experience to me until adulthood. Due to what I can only assume is magic, my children can run across deep snow, perfectly placing their weight so as not to sink. I, however, am not similarly skilled. No matter how hard I try, each step plunges me through the snow and to the frozen ground until I am knee deep and shivering.

In college, my husband thought it would be fun to jump off a ledge and into a snow berm. In his excitement, he underestimated how hard it would be to climb out. He sank up to his armpits and got stuck, much to the amusement of us watching. If it snows significantly in your area, then you understand just how difficult it is to move through snow like that. It requires your entire body to push against the weight of the snow and move forward.

I often find myself laughing at the trails I've left after endeavors such as these, the flailing legs and many falls chronicled in the snow behind me—often my full body outline where I dramatically fell to the ground and told my family to leave me and save themselves. It's been nearly a decade since I became an official

Washington resident, and I'm just now wising up. Instead of forging my own path through deep snow with heavy boots, struggling against the full weight of the snow alone, my journey could be made much easier if I simply followed someone who's gone before me (preferably with bigger boots).

The term "follower" has a negative connotation. Were you to describe someone this way, they'd most likely be offended. As a culture, we value leadership and belittle followers. There are countless classes, seminars, conferences, and summits dedicated to teaching leadership skills, raising up future leaders, and equipping companies to spot the leaders in their midst. Following, on the other hand, is looked down upon. From commercials to pop songs, we are constantly encouraged to go our own way and forge our own path. Children too have picked up on this idea, always vying for the coveted role at the front of the line during a game of "Following the Leader." Nobody wants to be labeled a follower. We all want to be leaders, and yet, as believers, following is exactly what we should be doing.

In John 12:26, Jesus says,

If anyone serves me, he must follow me;
and where I am, there will my servant be also.
If anyone serves me, the Father will honor him.

Perhaps part of the problem lies in our misunderstanding of the word "follow." Should you hear the word in America today, most likely it's in reference to social media. Facebook, Instagram, Twitter, TikTok, and Snapchat have taught us that "following" means observing someone from a distance, admiring their homes and hair, without actually knowing said person.

We browse, scroll, and filter through the lives of hundreds of people each day, expressing our approval with thumbs and hearts, never even brushing up against a real relationship, and call it "following."

Sometimes, if we really like what we see, we might even share some of their words or images with a cute little picture of a heart above it. We peruse and "like" often for hours a day and yet have no true interaction with the people we are following. Is it any wonder we often feel disconnected from the Lord? We've been following Him like we follow Taylor Swift and that just won't do.

Looking deeper at the Greek found in John 12, follow means "to follow one who precedes, join him as his attendant, accompany him," and "join one as one's disciple."[10] While Christ expects that we will observe through Scripture how He lived on earth and share His words with others, yes, if our interaction with Him stops there, we fall far short. Mark 8:34 says,

> *And calling the crowd to him with his disciples,*
> *he said to them,*
> *"If anyone would come after me,*
> *let him deny himself*
> *and take up his cross*
> *and follow me."*

At this point in Jesus' ministry, His reputation as a miracle worker was well established. Shortly before this, the crowd that was following Him had witnessed Him heal a blind man and feed four thousand hungry men (not to mention the women and children) with seven small loaves of bread. While certainly there

---

[10] Strongs G190

were those following Him with pure intentions, it is likely that the majority of the crowd were there for earthly gain—those with empty bellies, broken bodies, or simple curiosity. As He so often does, Jesus perceives and speaks to these, clarifying what following Him truly means. "Deny yourself," He says. "Deny yourself and take up your cross." In those seven words He both convicts and challenges us, convicting us of our innate selfishness and challenging us to set Him as the authority over our lives. While the idea of denying ourselves in favor of His will and heart is relatively easy for us to grasp today, the concept of taking up our cross is not a familiar one.

The crowds, however, knew just what He meant. In that time, a criminal sentenced to death by crucifixion would be required to carry his cross to the place of his death. This was a symbol, signifying that the condemned had come under the total authority of Rome.[11] The word picture used here is a heavy one. By asking us to deny ourselves and take up our cross, Christ has made it clear that following Him requires us to submit wholly to His authority, to His word, and to His leading, carrying our crosses to our very deaths. This is so much more than a social media following. This is a following that changes everything.

As we've seen, Mary Magdalene was a fantastic follower. She didn't simply admire Him from afar, but sacrificed everything in order to follow Him. She listened, learned, submitted, and obeyed. She denied herself daily and certainly carried the cross of His authority on her shoulders. Her life was devoted to the

---

[11] Barbieri, Lou. "Mark." In *The Moody Bible Commentary*, edited by Michael Rydelnik and Michael Vanlaningham, 1533. Chicago: Moody Publishers, 2014.

Messiah and it showed. But Mary didn't only follow. Mary also led. In the few mentions of Mary's life in Scripture, more than half of them connect her with other women.[12] In all of those verses, save one, Mary is listed first. The sole time Mary is named after others, she follows behind the mother and aunt of Jesus, honoring their relation to Christ.[13] This is significant. Mary's position at the front of the list implies that Mary was a well-respected woman, distinguished from the others by her faithfulness and loyalty. Walking closely with the women that followed Jesus, it is likely that she was revered among them. We can imagine her sharing her experiences with them, encouraging them with what she had seen and heard, and ultimately pointing them to Christ Himself. Yes, she followed Christ first and foremost, but even in her following, she led.

Joshua too was a follower. In Numbers 32:12, God describes him as a man who "wholly followed the Lord." His dedication to the Lord and obedience to His commands would be favored by God so much that he was one of only two people delivered from Egyptian slavery who would get to enter the Promised Land. All others would be barred for their rebellion against The Lord.[14]

We first meet Joshua in Exodus 17. Israel, recently rescued from slavery, is being attacked by the Amalekites. The Israelite leader, Moses, appoints Joshua to gather men and lead the fight against Amalek. Joshua

---

12 Lockyer, *All the Men/Women of the Bible Compilation SC*, 100
13 John 19:25
14 Numbers 32:11-12

obeys and helps bring victory to the Hebrew people—
a telling introduction to the man.

As he followed God, Joshua followed Moses. Moses
had a unique relationship to the Lord. He was the man
God chose to lead the nation of Israel out of Egypt and
through the wilderness. He alone knew the Lord face
to face.[15] He alone had the privilege of speaking to God
as a friend.[16] Surely Joshua recognized the special position Moses had with the Lord, for he stuck close to
Moses, taking up Moses' cause as his own.

The next time we meet Joshua in Scripture, he is operating as Moses' assistant, accompanying him to the
base of Mt. Sinai.[17] From there, Moses would travel up
the mountain to meet with God alone. Joshua would
wait at the bottom, following Moses as far as he could.
Like a toddler waiting for her mom to turn around before snatching candy out of the bowl, the Israelites left
without Moses would rebel against God.

Together, they made for themselves a golden calf to
raise up and worship.[18] Because he was following God
and Moses, Joshua had no part in this idolatry. Read
that again. Joshua's decision to follow would be the
very thing that kept him from sin, sparing him the consequences of a reckless act against The Lord. Joshua
would continue to follow Moses' lead throughout their
years in the wilderness, accompanying him even as he
met with the Lord in the tent of meeting.[19] Having
faithfully served alongside Moses, and thus the Lord,
throughout their wandering in the desert, Joshua

---

[15] Deuteronomy 34:10
[16] Exodus 33:11
[17] Exodus 24:13
[18] Exodus 32
[19] Exodus 33:11

would be chosen to lead the nation of Israel into the Promised Land after Moses' death. A great honor. A great responsibility.

Joshua, like Mary, was a follower first. He obeyed God's commands and followed His leading. He believed God and trusted in His guidance, and he followed God's appointed leader, Moses. Joshua was so devoted to following the Lord that he followed Moses to the base of Mt. Sinai, throughout the wilderness, and into the very tent where God was, and then, at the right time and in the right way, he led.

Contrary to what the world teaches, we are not created to be leaders, we are created to be followers, first God and then others. Like the deep snow that is so difficult to struggle through alone, the Christian life is much easier to navigate if we follow in the footsteps of someone who's ahead of us. In Titus 2:3-5, Paul gives instructions for older women, though hidden in the passage are instructions for younger women as well. Let's look.

> *Older women likewise are to be reverent in behavior,*
> *not slanderers or slaves to much wine.*
> *They are to teach what is good,*
> *and so train the young women to love their husbands and children,*
> *to be self-controlled, pure, working at home, kind, and submissive to their own husbands,*
> *that the word of God may not be reviled.*

Did you catch it? It's subtle, but it's there. If older women are to teach younger women how to follow Christ, then younger women are to listen and learn. Older women are to lead and younger women are to follow. It's that simple. In this stage of life, are you the older woman or the younger? Trick question—you're both. Each of us are further along in our walk with the Lord than someone and each of us are behind someone as well. Paul gives us instructions for how to navigate both kinds of relationships. Follow and lead. Teach and learn.

Hebrews 13:7 says,

Remember your leaders,
Those who spoke to you the word of God.
Consider the outcome of their way of life,
And imitate their faith.

As women, we tend to think we have to do it all alone. We add item upon item onto our to-do lists until we find ourselves burnt out, overwhelmed, and frazzled. In this harried state, we can no longer do our jobs well, love our families well, or still worse, honor our God well. Scripture offers us hope. In the final chapter of Hebrews, the writer instructs us to consider the lives of our leaders and imitate their faith. Is there someone that is a bit further ahead of you, living a faithful life of integrity? Follow her! Sit at her feet. Seek her counsel. Ask for her help and heed her advice. We don't lose any points in the game of life by imitating the good habits of another woman of God. If anything, we gain them by avoiding needless mistakes and missteps.

There are women in our churches ahead of us on the snowy path of life. They have wisdom to offer and hope to pass on. As we lean into our role as both the younger and older women, soon enough we won't just be following anymore. We will also be leading, reaching our hands back to help the younger women behind us navigate the berms. If we all took the instructions in Titus 2 seriously, we'd find ourselves with a seemingly endless line of women helping each other along, following after Christ. The impossible-to-pass snow would quickly seem much more possible as feet after feet trample it down, making way for the next generation of believers. The apostle Paul puts it this way, "Follow me as I follow Christ."[20] Paul understood that he was first a follower of Christ; but just as he followed the path laid before him by the Son of God, so Paul left a path behind, ready to be followed.

Women who are present in Christ's life must follow first. We must be women who are committed to following hard after the Lord, no matter how many disruptions come our way, seeking guidance and encouragement through the Word daily. We follow when the path is well trodden and well lit. We follow when the path takes us through deep snow, laboring against it with all our might. We follow while it is still dark and we feel all alone. We must follow, and in our following, we will leave a trail ready to be picked up by any who come behind us as they seek hard after Him. Like Mary. Like Joshua. Like Paul. Follow me, I'm following Christ.

Go Deeper:

1. Do you have an older woman of God helping you follow Christ? If so, take the time to write her a letter today, thanking her for the gift of her time, her wisdom, and her encouragement. If not, write out a prayer asking God to bring a mentor into your life.

---

[20] 1 Corinthians 11:1

2. Do you have a younger woman that you are pointing to Christ? If so, write out a letter to her encouraging her in her walk with the Lord. If not, write out a prayer asking the Lord to reveal whom He would have you serve.

Chapter 4

Present in Christ's Death, We Endure

When I was just nineteen years old, my younger brother ran into a lake, dove under the water, and hit his hands on a hidden sand bank. The resulting whiplash broke his neck, paralyzing him immediately and causing him to drown. Miraculously, he survived. After three months in the ICU, one month in step-down, countless surgeries and procedures, and too many hours spent fighting to survive, he came home. Over a decade later, contrary to all the doctors' opinions, he is still with us, though to this day he remains paralyzed from the neck down and ventilator dependent.

I'm not sure you're ever ready for a day like that day—the day everything changes. I remember where I was when the phone rang. I remember the way the sun looked when we walked into the hospital for the first time. I remember the frantic way nurses and techs moved around my brother as we entered his room. I remember collapsing on the floor as sorrow flooded over me. I remember feeling abandoned. I remember questioning it all.

For some reason, Sunday school classes don't often cover suffering. Odd, isn't it? We teach children about Noah's ark and the crucifixion but somehow separate it from ourselves, as if the hard parts of life aren't for us to experience. We create cute songs about Abraham and Jonah, and sweeten their stories to make them fun and adorable, but we don't tell the whole truth. We leave out the important parts—the parts that make all the difference on days like that day, the day my brother drowned.

Each and every one of us will face difficulty in this life. We will be confronted with hard things. We will be stretched until we think we will break. We will be rejected and hurt time and again, but contrary to what we are often taught, this is exactly what's expected of believers.

Somehow, we've accepted the lie that following Jesus means signing ourselves up for the good life, one free of bumps and bruises, offenses and ordeals; and yet, this is precisely what Jesus promised us. We will be asked to endure trying things, but not because God has forgotten us. We will be asked to endure because we are meant to endure. John 16:33 says,

> *I have said these things to you,*
> *That in me you may have peace.*
> *In the world you will have tribulation.*
> *But take heart;*
> *I have overcome the world.*

I came to cherish this verse while my brother was in the hospital. I recited it to myself, painted it onto canvas, and clung to it with every ounce of determination I had left. Is it any wonder this passage became so dear to me during that time? When my world fell apart, how comforting it was to be reminded that the world was no match for Jesus. I can't help but wonder, however, how much more beneficial this passage would have been before the tragedy struck—not only as a reminder of what Christ has done, but as a promise of what's to come for believers—a promise we rarely want to face.

Mary Magdalene faced tribulation in her life. In fact, tribulation could be described as her near-constant companion. As we know, Mary spent a portion of her life under the oppression of seven demons until Christ set her free. We've discussed just how devastating that oppression must have been for Mary and just how sweet her rescue must have felt.

Though her darkest chapter closed at the sound of His voice, this was not the end of her struggle. No, meeting Jesus did not automatically offer her a pain-free life. Sometime later, she would watch helplessly as her Rescuer was brutally killed. She would mourn and question and struggle with her grief and fear until one morning, she would meet Him again.

While our interaction with Mary in Scripture ends shortly after this meeting, we can assume her trials did not. Jesus' disciples went on to face incredible difficulties in their lives. Many were imprisoned, beaten, and killed for sharing the good news of the Gospel. So too, we can imagine Mary faced many very real struggles as she continued to tell others about the resurrection. Certainly, she watched as her friends navigated intense persecution. Most assuredly did she mourn the loss of some of her most cherished loved ones. Oh yes, Mary endured much.

Somewhere throughout our history, the American church has come to believe that struggle, though typical of the apostles' experience, is not actually in God's plans for His people. We read the accounts and letters and then close them up, relegating them to a time long past and a purpose long changed. We let the Bible stories remain in the pages and convince ourselves that the apostles' experiences as they followed Christ must be atypical, a product of their culture and time. "Nothing like that will happen to believers today," we console ourselves. But that is a lie. A total and complete lie. The apostles' experience is not the exception, but the rule.

Consider the book of Hebrews. Through an unknown author, the Holy Spirit inspired this letter to encourage a particular group of Christians. These men and women were Jewish by birth, but had converted to Christianity sometime before the letter was written. Having faced persecution for their faith, many of them were considering leaving Christianity and returning once more to Judaism. The author writes to encourage them not to return to the former way, but to hold fast the course—as Jesus is better than anything the old ways had to offer.

While we don't know much more about the recipients or the author, the timeline of the letter is enough to give us some insight as to what these believers were facing. Hebrews was likely written shortly before 70 AD, during Nero's reign over the Roman Empire.[21] Dubbed by John Foxe as "The First Persecution", Nero's attempt to exterminate the Christians was cruel and horrific.

After killing his family and senators, he ordered the city of Rome to be lit aflame and burned continually

---

[21] Sauer, Ronald. "Hebrews." In *The Moody Bible Commentary*, edited by Michael Rydelnik and Michael Vanlaningham, 1921. Chicago: Moody Publishers, 2014.

for nearly seven days.[22] In an altogether chilling move, Nero blamed the fire on none other than the Christians, and began further persecuting them. Nero's persecution was intense. Among other atrocities, he was known to dip believers in wax, hang them from trees, and set them on fire to light his gardens. He would sew them into animal skins while they were living and set dogs to attack them until they succumbed to their wounds. Imagine what it must have been like for Christians during this time. Believers were being killed at an alarming rate, and in devastating ways—and the Hebrews were terrified.

In light of this, it is easy to see why this letter was necessary. This was the world in which the recipients of this letter lived. Can you see why they might have considered leaving Christianity and going back to the safety of Judaism? Men and woman of God around them were literally being burned alive and eaten by dogs, how overwhelmingly frightening that must have been! And yet, the writer does something shocking. Instead of validating, sympathizing, or coddling these believers, the writer affirms their experience as normal, altogether expected, and wholly ordinary.

In Hebrews chapter 11, the author writes a marvelous account of men and women who have gone before us and remained faithful in the midst of extreme trial. Often called "The Hall of Faith," this list is not simply a sweet summarization or heroic history, it's a call to action—a call to endure. At the end of chapter ten, the writer reminds the recipients that they had already endured hardship when they first came to faith and provokes them to continue pressing on by stating that,

---

[22] John Foxe, *Foxe's Book of Martyrs* (Grand Rapids: Baker Books, 2001), 5

"we are not of those who shrink back and are destroyed, but of those who have faith and preserve their souls."[23] The hall of faith is placed immediately after this statement, proving the author's point with a magnificent compilation of believers who have done just that—held the faith and preserved their souls in the midst of trial and difficulty, all the way to the end.

While the list alone is enough to bring renewed vigor and resolve, the author doesn't leave us here. In chapter 12:1-2 he states,

> *Therefore, since we are surrounded by so great a cloud of witnesses, let us also lay aside every weight, and sin which clings so closely, and let us run with endurance the race that is set before us, looking to Jesus, the founder and perfecter of our faith, who for the joy that was set before him endured the cross, despising the shame, and is seated at the right hand of the throne of God.*

In these two verses, the author reiterates his point—we can endure because these past believers endured; or better, we can endure, because He endured. Remember when we said that following Christ means following believers who have gone before us? This doesn't exclude suffering. We don't get to follow Christ in all His triumph and glory and none of His pain, rejection, and distress. As much as we'd like it, that's not how this works. We don't get to pick and choose what parts of His life we follow—it's all or nothing. In fact, Romans 8:16-17 puts this in plain language.

---

[23] Hebrews 10:39

The Spirit himself bears witness with our spirit that we are children of God, and if children, then heirs—heirs of God and fellow heirs with Christ, provided we suffer with him in order that we may also be glorified with him.

The suffering and the glory go hand in hand. They cannot be separated. We are heirs of the glory won by Christ, eternal life in Heaven with Him, if we follow Him in His suffering. That's the deal. We can take it or leave it, but we don't get to negotiate the terms.

Let's look at Christ. If we are to share in His suffering, we best understand what we can expect. As an infant, Jesus was already a wanted man. King Herod of Judea, threatened by the coming of another king, desired Jesus killed immediately. So determined was he to preserve his throne that he ordered all the boys in the region around Christ's birth two years old and younger to be put to death. Jesus' parents, due to the warning of an angel, had already fled to Egypt and escaped Herod's wicked plan.[24] Jesus survives to live a relatively ordinary life of which we know very little until sometime around his thirtieth year.[25] This is the point in His life in which He begins ministering to the people around Him. Once again, Jesus draws the attention of all the wrong people. Proclaiming Himself to be the Son of God and God Himself, the Pharisees seek His death for apparent blasphemy.

Though we know Christ's claims to be true, claiming to be God was enough to earn you death at this time, and the Pharisees could not accept Christ's message of hope and life. They did not have eyes to see,

---

[24] Matthew 2
[25] Luke 3:23

and thus sought to kill Him. During His ministry, Jesus would visit His hometown but would not be able to perform many miracles because those He grew up with could not accept Him as God either.[26] He was laughed at,[27] accused of using demonic forces,[28] criticized for just about everything He did—including who He chose to spend time with.[29] Ultimately, He was rejected by the very people He came to save. Very little of His life was easy or comfortable but all of it was good. This is what we can look forward to in this life— rejection, struggle, hurt—and all for the glory of God.

Being present in Christ's death means we get to endure hardships just as Christ endured hardships. We get to be rejected for the sake of the gospel, we get to struggle against the weight of this fallen world, we get to carry light into dark places and plant our feet firmly on the ground as the powers of evil attempt to tear down the hope that we have been given. Being present in Christ's death means we will be hurt by the same world that so desperately hated Jesus, and we get to consider it an honor because sharing in His suffering means sharing in His glory—and that's all we could ever desire.

While my brother was fighting for his life, a friend made t-shirts for us with Isaiah 40:30-31 printed on them. Here's what they read:

> *Youths may become faint and weary,*
> *and young men stumble and fall,*
> *but those who trust in the Lord*
> *will renew their strength;*

---

[26] Matthew 13:53-58
[27] Matthew 9:24
[28] Matthew 9:34, 12:24; Luke 11:15
[29] Luke 15:2, 19:7

they will soar on wings like eagles;
they will run and not become weary,
they will walk and not faint.

This passage was written to the faithful among the nation of Israel, reminding them that God will continue to work out His purposes through them even when everything seems like it's falling apart and to encourage them to remain steadfast in the midst of chaos.[30] It was a fitting passage for that time in my family's life, as everything was uncertain and we were finding ourselves questioning the goodness of God and His ultimate purpose daily. Only later did the image of a soaring eagle really hit me.

Our home in Washington is on a hill near a lake, providing a prime spot for enjoying the many incredible birds in the area. Though our property is landlocked, we once found a large fish in our backyard, apparently fumbled by a bird of prey and plopped to it's final resting spot next to our fire pit. Sitting on the porch, I often spot bald eagles flying overhead. Each time I stop what I am doing and choose instead to admire their beauty and their grace. One such time, I noticed just how little these birds flap their wings. Curious, I decided to look it up.

According to Jon M. Gerrard and Gary R. Bortolotti, bald eagles actively flap their wings for an average of two minutes per hour.[31] The rest of the time, they are simply soaring. That's an extraordinary fact! When

---

[30] Rydelnik, Michael; Spencer, James. "Isaiah." In *The Moody Bible Commentary*, edited by Michael Rydelnik and Michael Vanlaningham, 1533. Chicago: Moody Publishers, 2014.

[31] Bortolotti, Gary R.; Gerrard, Jon M. The Bald Eagle: Haunts and Habits of a Wilderness Monarch. Washington D.C., Smithsonian Books, 1988.

Scripture tells us that those who trust in the Lord will soar on wings like eagles, the implications of this are huge. While it takes extraordinary effort to flap eagles' massive wings, in order to fly successfully they only have to flap for a short amount of time. After that, they simply let the wind carry them.

As believers present in Christ's death, we are asked to endure extraordinary things for the glory of God. Our initial decision to trust the Lord in the midst of trial is our version of active flapping. We too muster all the strength we can manage to get ourselves going. We choose, often against everything we feel and see, to keep believing that God is good and is working in our favor. And just like the birds, our meager efforts are enough. As the wind carries the birds fifty-eight minutes out of an hour, so too The Lord will carry us once we enter the skies of belief. Our ability to endure is far less about how much we can withstand or how mentally tough we are and far more about Who we are trusting. Imagine an eagle deciding it didn't trust the air to carry them and instead kept furiously flapping away. Were the eagles to attempt to flap their wings the entirety of an hour, they'd likely run out of energy before ever reaching their destination. It would be futile effort. In fact, we'd probably laugh at the poor eagle. *Don't you realize you were created to soar? Your wings were built with this specific purpose in mind! Take advantage of it,* we'd think. The thing is, this is what we often do to ourselves. We decide that the Lord can't be trusted to carry us and attempt to carry ourselves, failing miserably along the way. Trusting that The Lord will carry us in the darkest parts of your life is hard, nobody will tell you otherwise, but it's also exactly how we were created. When you find yourself flapping away, attempting to muscle yourself through the latest trial or struggle, remember that you were meant to rely on the Lord. Remember that your wings were built for it. Remember Who you are trusting, and endure.

Go Deeper:

1. What are you being asked to endure today? Did Christ experience something similar?

2. Are you attempting to work your way through this struggle on your own strength or are you surrendering yourself to God's working in your life?

3. Read through Hebrews 11. Whose endurance stands out to you most? Why?

Chapter 5

Present in Christ's Death, We Obey

My first two children are two years apart, both born in May. We call them our Maybies. Each of them arrived around a week before their respective due-dates, so when we found out we were expecting our third in late April, I figured we had broken the streak. No more Maybies for us. My youngest, however, has been strong-willed from the womb and already had a mind of her own. She hung in there, insisting that she not be left out from all the May fun to be had, arriving late and just sneaking into May.

After what seemed like years of walking, bouncing, and eating all the pineapple to this very tired mama, our youngest came into the world quickly and intensely—and boom, we had three Maybies. Little did I know at the time, her entrance into the world was entirely indicative of her personality. She is her own human. She is not easily swayed. She knows exactly what she wants and how she wants it done. She is unyielding, and we love her for it. Those traits will serve her well as she seeks to follow hard after Christ, I'm absolutely convinced of it. As a toddler, however, those same traits could be quite challenging.

When she was not yet three, we met some friends at a park. This wasn't simply a park, but a sports complex. It had basketball courts, a skate park, BMX track, baseball and soccer fields, as well as the usual playgrounds and splash pads. As it had plenty of space to run, clean bathrooms, and abundant sun, we often packed a picnic and spent the entire day there.

One such day, I was feeling particularly pleased with myself as my youngest had actually let me do her hair (miracle number one) and had worn the cutest little romper I had picked out for her (miracle number two). I had considered that day a win, and maybe even allowed myself to dream of future days without a toddler refusing all hygiene and any outfit that matches, fits, and is weather appropriate.

My daughter was clean, dressed appropriately, and was thus far compliant—maybe I was getting this parenting gig under control after all. But no, she was just biding her time. Now, this child is a runner. All moms know the type—the kid that when confronted will simply bolt in the opposite direction, leaving a trail of parents and shoes behind in the wake of their maniacal laughter. This girl did not like to be told "no," or even, "not yet," and would simply flee the scene in an effort to find the freedom to live as she pleased. She never achieved her independence, but she successfully wore me out 100% of the time.

We had been at the park about an hour when it happened. Little miss had started to drift further and further away from the playground, one little step at a time, when I realized that she was attempting escape. Wary of startling her into a full-on run, I moved one foot towards her and simply said her name, hoping that she would come right back when called. But it was too late. She had tasted freedom and she thirsted for more. With fire in her eyes, she smiled at me and, in one seamless move, flung the straps of her romper off her shoulders, stepped out of it, and took off naked down the soccer fields. My friends and many strangers enjoyed the show as I hauled myself after her as she laughed her pull-uped bottom off, finally wrestling her back into her clothes behind a netted soccer goal.

Reflecting back on that day, I can't help but see myself in that tiny red-headed toddler. You see, that morning she looked as if she and I were in sync—her hair was done, she was well dressed, and was even wearing shoes (miracle number three). She looked the part, until she stripped it all off and ran in the other direction. She had never been operating out of true obedience. She had simply played along until it didn't suit her anymore. While the sight of the nearly-nude red-head running down the soccer fields was enough to make anyone laugh, it has stuck with me for an altogether different reason—true obedience cannot simply be outward, it must originate from the heart.

We are not born obedient. It's something we have to learn, and learn again. As people, our nature is to question authority and trust our own gut, just like my streaking ginger. We don't like to be told what to do, how to do it, or even when to do it. We want to control as much as possible, even going so far as choosing to go the opposite way as an authority figure simply because we don't want to be perceived as submissive. As Christ followers, however, we must be able to obey. Again, this isn't a trendy part of Christianity. You won't find celebrities raving about the new life path of obedience to God they're on. This isn't going to sweep the nation as the newest TikTok challenge. This won't suddenly start trending on Instagram, but in reality, it should.

At this moment, #bestlife has 2.6 million posts and #liveyourbestlife has 3.3 million posts on Instagram. A quick survey of those would lead women to believe that our best lives our spent posing in swimsuits in exotic locations and eating gourmet food while wearing all the makeup. Conversely, #obedientlife has less than 100 posts—usually filled with Scripture or testimonies of submission to God and the goodness He gives in return. With more than 100 million posts per day, less than 100 total posts with #obedientlife is hardly substantial. This isn't popular. It's not flashy. What's ironic, however, is that #liveyourbestlife and #obedientlife are actually the same thing—but the world won't tell you that. In fact, the world wants you to believe anything but that.

There are two kinds of obedience that are worth exploring—obedience to His word and obedience to His prompting. Though both are equally important, I would argue that we cannot discern the Lord's prompting without first knowing the word, so let's start there, in that beautiful book given to us straight from God.

Earlier, we discovered the importance of setting aside time to meet the Lord in prayer and the word. We discussed the vital role Scripture plays in equipping us for the good works set before us and just how important it is to make daily Bible reading a priority. All of this is true and good and very worthwhile, but it must not end there. We cannot simply read the Bible every day. We also have to do what it says. Contemplate what Christ said about obedience.

> *If you keep my commandments,*
> *you will abide in my love,*
> *just as I have kept my Father's commandments*

and abide in his love.
John 15:10

"Whoever has my commandments and keeps them, he it is who loves me. And he who loves me will be loved by my Father, and I will love him and manifest myself to him." Judas (not Iscariot) said to him, "Lord, how is it that you will manifest yourself to us, and not to the world?" Jesus answered him, "If anyone loves me, he will keep my word, and my Father will love him, and we will come to him and make our home with him. Whoever does not love me does not keep my words. And the word that you hear is not mine but the Father who sent me."
John 14:21-24

Blessed rather are those who hear the word of God and keep it!
Luke 11:28

Truly, truly, I say to you, if anyone keeps my word, he will never see death.
John 8:51

Jesus' own words testify to the importance of obedience. After His resurrection, when He is commissioning the disciples to go out and tell the world about Him, He doesn't just implore them to teach the good news. He requires them to teach others to obey! It's of utmost importance! Obedience is how we show we love the Father. It's the invitation to Christ to make His home with us. It's the key to abiding in the Father's love. In fact, John later writes that we will know whether or not we are truly saved by whether or not we obey. Observe the intensity of John's writing:

*And by this we know that we have come to know him,
if we keep his commandments. Whoever says "I
know him" but does not keep his commandments is a
liar, and the truth is not in him, but whoever keeps
his word, in him truly the love of God is perfected. By
this we may know that we are in him: whoever says
he abides in him ought to walk in the same way in
which he walked.*
1 John 2:3-6

It is critical that we note here that obedience is
never a means to salvation. God, and God alone, brings
that about based solely on grace through faith. We cannot work our way into heaven or earn our salvation
solely by being a good person; obedience is a mark of
that salvation. Once we have been set apart by grace
through faith, we should find ourselves more and
more able to obey God's commands in Scripture. Our
desire to obey should be ever increasing and we
should find it easier and easier to keep ourselves from
sin. This is the natural outworking of the Holy Spirit in
the life of a believer. What a relief that is! As a believer
present in Christ's death, we will be women who obey
the word and take joy in doing so!

The second form of obedience is obedience to God's
prompting. While Scripture is the primary way God
speaks to us today, He is still prompting us on an individual level to be faithful to His calling on our lives. I
once told God I would never go to Moody Bible Institute. I was adamant that that was not the place for me,
and yet, when it came time to apply for college, I knew,
deeply knew, that Moody was where God was leading
me. Now, there is no verse in the Bible that said,
"Joélle, you must go to Moody." That's not how it

works, even though it would be lovely and oh-so-convenient.

Rather, my time spent in Scripture had taught me to recognize the voice of the Lord in my very soul. As believers, He indwells us—giving us the Holy Spirit to illuminate Scripture and call to mind passages right when we need them. God also will give us wisdom when we ask for it and guide us to the path He has chosen for us, if only we are willing to pay attention. But that starts in the word—learning and discerning Who He Is and how He moves. No wonder our time in the Bible is so important. It accomplishes so many goals all at once!

Jesus Himself tells us that His children will discern His voice and follow Him.[32] It's one of the many benefits to having a true, salvific relationship with Christ— we get His help and wisdom as we navigate our lives. This is no small thing! He actually wants to speak into our lives and lead us in the paths of righteousness. He will prompt us and encourage us and enable us to follow Him, all we have to do is obey! And yet, obedience is often difficult, especially in an era that considers "submission" a dirty word.

Too often we think like my then two-year-old. We think submission to authority and the subsequent obedience will rob us of all our joy, identity, and personality. We may try it out for a bit, wearing submission like a romper and shoes, until we finally discard them and run our own way. But herein lies the problem. The problem isn't with submission, the problem is with us. We don't buy in, and because of that, we find obedience to be stifling and draining, rather than life-

---

[32] John 10:27

giving. But this is never the way it was intended. In John 10:10, Jesus says,

The thief comes only to steal and kill and destroy. I came that they may have life and have it abundantly.

Maybe you're thinking, "Wait a second. Didn't we just read about how Jesus requires us to obey? How can we now say He wants us to have an abundant life?"

You're not alone. Many of us struggle to see how the obedient life and the abundant life go hand in hand. When we come to a disconnect between what we see in Scripture and what we see in our lives, Scripture trumps all. If we read these statements of Jesus and think that they contradict each other, we have no choice but to think again, because if Jesus said it, it's true no matter what. So, how can this be? How can abundance come from obedience, a literal submission of our will for that of another?

Remember that time I told God I would never go to Moody Bible Institute, only to find that Moody was exactly where He would have me go? That seemingly small act of obedience affected more than I could ever have imagined. To save time, I'll simply highlight the big ones. Had I not been obedient to the Lord, I would not have received the Bible and theology training that kept me afloat the months following my brother's drowning. Had I not been obedient to the Lord, I would have never gotten the counseling training that allowed me to better serve my family after my brother came home. Had I not been obedient, I would have never met my now husband. Had I not been obedient, I would have never been gifted my incredible in-laws. Had I not been obedient, I would not be the mother to my three biological children. Had I not been obedient,

I would never have gotten to mother twelve children through Safe Families for Children. And had I not been obedient in something as trivial as where I went to college, I would not have known The Lord as intimately as I do. Further acts of obedience in my life have unlocked astonishingly good gifts from the Father and increasing abundance out of submission.

Note what I didn't say. I did not say that my obedience brought about material gain. I did not say that obedience brought about a life free from pain. I did not say that obedience brought about a struggle-free existence. None of that would be true, but I did say that obedience would bring about further goodness from the Lord and (spoiler alert) further calls to obedience.

All of the good gifts given by God through that one act of obedience required me to further submit myself to the King of Kings. Marriage and parenthood require me to selflessly lay down myself for others daily (hourly). Taking in children of families in crisis increases that submission exponentially. Knowing the Bible as I do requires me to share that knowledge with others. Obedience leads to the abundant life in Christ, yes, but perhaps more notably it leads to further chances to obey.

Don't take my word for it, take the Word for it. Scripture attests to this truth continually. We've seen just how faithful a follower Mary Magdalene was—she obediently answered the call of the Lord on her life. As she followed Jesus, no doubt her responsibilities increased—more opportunities to share the gospel, serve the Christ, and submit her desires for that of His. Obedience begot obedience.

Consider Joseph, Jesus' earthly father. During their year-long betrothal, the Holy Spirit brings about pregnancy in Mary. Determined in his mind to divorce Mary quietly, Joseph is met by an angel of the Lord in a dream telling him the truth about Mary's pregnancy and imploring him to continue with the marriage, for this Child would be the long-awaited Savior.[33] Do not gloss over the cultural implications of this.

During this time, much more than today, a baby born before marriage was something that would bring much shame upon a family. Joseph choosing to continue with the betrothal rather than demanding a divorce would imply his participation in the pregnancy, and ultimately his guilt. In order to preserve his good name, it would seem reasonable and even compassionate for him to quietly bow out of the marriage, even with this new information. But this is not what Joseph did. Joseph chose the way of obedience. Matthew 1:24-25 says,

When Joseph woke from sleep, he did as the angel of the Lord commanded him: he took his wife, but knew her not until she had given birth to a son. And he called his name Jesus.

When Joseph awoke from meeting the angel of the Lord, he immediately set in his heart to obey God completely. He carried the responsibility of marrying Mary and protecting the integrity of the pregnancy so absolutely, that he abstained from sexual intimacy with Mary, even after their marriage was official, until Jesus was born. What remarkable obedience! While the world might view the obedience of Joseph as foolishness, his surrendering of his will for God's was not

---

[33] Matthew 1:18-23

without reward. This act of submission to the Lord, though assuredly difficult, would allow Joseph a unique spot in the life of the Messiah—a privilege he would have missed had he disobeyed and gone his own way.

Joseph's call to obedience didn't end there. Two more times an angel of the Lord would appear to Joseph, requiring him to take action.[34] Two more times Joseph would obey. Each and every call to obedience on Joseph's life would cost something of him, but each and every call would lead him further into relationship with God, the Messiah, and his wife. Abundance out of obedience, time and time again.

Jesus Himself modeled obedience perfectly. His example stands for us to follow today. Philippians 2:5-11 says,

> *Adopt the same attitude as that of Christ Jesus,*
> *who, existing in the form of God,*
> *did not consider equality with God*
> *as something to be exploited.*
> *Instead he emptied himself*
> *by assuming the form of a servant,*
> *taking on the likeness of humanity.*
> *And when he had come as a man,*
> *he humbled himself by becoming obedient*
> *to the point of death—*
> *even to death on a cross.*
> *For this reason God highly exalted him*
> *and gave him the name*
> *that is above every name,*
> *so that at the name of Jesus*
> *every knee will bow—*

---

[34] Matthew 2:13, 20

in heaven and on earth
and under the earth—
and every tongue will confess
that Jesus Christ is Lord,
to the glory of God the Father.[35]

Christ's extreme obedience on the cross led to His exaltation and created a way for men and women to live eternally with Him. Because of His obedience through His death, there will come a day when every man, woman, and child will proclaim that He is Lord, giving all glory to God our Father. Abundance out of obedience. Paul, the author of Philippians, goes on to urge the Philippians to continue to obey just as Christ obeyed. His attitude should be our attitude. Joseph adopted this same attitude when he submitted his will to that of The Father's, choosing instead to bear the scorn of marrying a woman pregnant before marriage. While we are only told that the angel of the Lord appeared to him three times, no doubt Joseph's obedience was not limited to these instances. Surely, he was led by the Lord to serve his family time and time again, and surely each time cost him something—whether time, rest, or energy. Joseph chose the way of obedience and was better for it.

As we seek to be present in Christ's death, we will be women of obedience. We will submit to Scripture and the Lord's leading in our lives, knowing that through our obedience God is working out His ultimate plan. As we are faithful to obey, we can rest in the truth that He will give us an abundant life—abundant in Himself, in truth, and in eternity.

---

[35] Christian Standard Bible

When my daughter was asked to obey on that sunny day years ago, she obliged for a short time, but her heart was never in it. She couldn't see that my direction to her was for her wellbeing—brushing her hair to keep it from getting too tangled, putting on clothes and shoes to protect her body from sun and injury. To her, submission was surrendering too much, when in reality, submission meant being given safety. We too often see obedience to the Lord as surrendering parts of ourselves that seem like the very parts that make us "us." Although we don't like to admit it, sometimes our sins are so ingrained in us that giving them up may feel like giving up our very personalities. Who would I be if I didn't watch that show? What would I have in common with my friends if I didn't read those books or listen to that music? Would my boyfriend still love me if I moved out? If we stopped having sex? Would my coworkers like me if I stopped complaining about our boss? What will my friends say if I don't get drunk with them on the weekends? How will I cope with my life if I'm sober? Unfortunately, the enemy can easily convince us that our sinful selves are our true selves. He tells us that stifling these desires will lead to unhappiness and pain, that obedience is inauthentic and that true joy will never be found by denying what we want in the moment. Nothing could be further from the truth. When we believe in the Lord Jesus Christ as our Savior, the sinful self-dies and we are given power over sin. Walking in that power and letting the Holy Spirit lead us into our new life as Christ followers is the most authentic and life-giving thing we can do!

Sometimes we avoid obedience in an effort to be relatable. We convince ourselves that the best way to share the gospel is by showing the world that we aren't that different from them after all. We want people to see us as "real," but "real" is only helpful if it points others to Jesus. Too often "real" is just code for pointing others to ourselves—proving that we aren't like other Christians, that we can be fun and cool and non-judgmental while simultaneously offering the lost nothing but fond memories and empty hopes.

We avoid obedience and call it avoiding legalism, when in reality, we just don't like how conviction feels. We don't want to be perceived as stuffy or judgmental and understand that so many have been hurt by an American church that leaned heavily towards legalism for so long, that we run the other direction—straight into sin's waiting arms. We must define our terms. Legalism is ensuring others act in accordance with my beliefs. Integrity is ensuring that I do. It's an important distinction. When we mistake integrity for legalism, we take ourselves out of submission to the Father and place ourselves once again as sole authority—idolatry at its very basic level.

An important note—we won't always be obedient to God's Word. In fact, many times we will fall far short, hurting ourselves and hurting others. In those times, it's important to be apologizing people. Being able to say clearly, "I was wrong. I am sorry. Will you forgive me?" is of vital importance to building the Kingdom of Heaven here on this earth. Try as you might, you will hurt people. No matter how noble or holy your intentions, we are going to make mistakes and people will be offended. In those moments, we must be quick to own up to our sins, apologize, and ask forgiveness—even when you think they should just suck it up. Even when you "did everything right." Even when your intentions are good. When we hurt some-one around us, we apologize right away because rela-tionship is more important than being right, and right-eousness is more important than feeling righteous.

Women who are present in Christ's death will strive to follow Him in obedience. Unlike my daughter, whose straps of obedience grew itchy and uncomfort-able, we will be able to see obedience as the true gift it is, wearing it joyfully and contentedly. When we have a proper understanding of what submission is and does, out of our hearts will flow obedience, and through that obedience God will give us more and more of Himself.

Go Deeper:

1. What areas of your life do you find it easiest to obey God? What areas are the hardest?

2. Pick one area of your life in which obedience has not come easily. Write it down and stick it some-where visible (refrigerator, mirror, etc.). Each time you see it, take thirty seconds to ask God to give you a joyfully obedient heart in that area.

3. Ask a friend to commit to praying with you for a heart that delights in obedience. Commit to pray for that friend as well.

Chapter 6

Present in Christ's Death, We Remember

Shortly after my eighteenth birthday, I decided to get my first tattoo. At that time, I was just beginning my years at Moody Bible Institute and was struggling through the transition to being on my own, thousands of miles from my family. Wanting to remind myself that even in the midst of upheaval God remained constant and unchanging, I chose a pi symbol and planted it permanently on my wrist. Just over a year later, in the throes of seeming hopelessness after my brother's accident, I spotted "elpis" in one of my textbooks. Elpis is the word for "hope" in biblical Greek—specifically the hope that we have of eternal life in Christ Jesus. Wouldn't you know it, right in the middle sits the letter pi. It didn't take long before I was back in the chair, finishing that beautiful word on my wrist. Ever since that day, I have had a permanent reminder of our constant and unchanging hope written on my arm, visible for all to see.

Many believers have similar stories of tattoos chosen during tumultuous times to remind us of the truth of Who God Is and what He's promised to do. Other times we choose tattoos as reminders of what He has already done. Either way, we've chosen permanent displays of things that need to be remembered. On the other hand, many believers choose to remember the truth of Scripture in ways that involve fewer needles (understandably).

I once heard of a family that took the time to write on a stone each time they saw God move. They would then place the stone in their garden, creating a visible reminder of the many times God had worked on their behalf. When they needed to recall, they simply snatched a rock from the collection and read the story out loud. Similarly, my sister-in-law journals daily— three things she is grateful for and three prayer requests. As the pages turn so too does God's provision in her life, forever recorded for herself and her family. Others wear specific jewelry to keep the truth close or link certain songs with specific times that God has moved. Whatever the method, the reasoning is always the same—the most important things must not be forgotten, even if sometimes, they're the easiest to let slip.

With the cushion of millennia between us, and the crucifixion, it's easy to miss how devastating that weekend must have been for Jesus' followers. At most, believers since have had to live mere seconds after hearing of Christ's brutal death before learning of the resurrection. For those of us alive today, we can't separate the horror of Friday without the victory of Sunday. For Jesus' followers, that horror was all they had for nearly two full days. Imagine for a moment what it must have been like for Jesus' disciples. While the disciples certainly expected the coming of the Messiah, people during that time would not have expected a carpenter from Nazareth. Instead, they were looking for an earthly king, someone noble and magnificent.

The coming Messiah was anticipated as a glorious and mighty ruler, one that would establish a kingdom immediately. No doubt many of the followers of Jesus were awaiting that "gotcha moment" when Jesus would throw off His lowly robes in exchange for some fit for royalty, overthrowing the Roman government and taking His rightful place on the throne. While certainly Jesus will rule over the earth once again, there was work to be done first—work His followers did not anticipate. With this perspective, the crucifixion must have been completely devastating and totally distressing at best. From where they stood, the great plan of God had been disrupted—foiled by an angry mob and religious leaders. With the death of their teacher, they were most likely frightened, confused, and overwhelmed. The leaders at the time had determined that Jesus was a threat worth eliminating by any means possible. It was completely reasonable to expect they would be coming for His disciples next. That Saturday after His death must have been their darkest day yet.

As a worried pre-teen, I scribbled the promises of God on construction paper with cut and pasted photos of zoo animals next to them and taped them to my bedroom walls. While I no longer include pictures of tigers and elephants, I still find myself hanging handwritten verses in my home when I need reminding. If you're anything like me, difficult situations leave you frantically searching Scripture for any sign of hope. I tear through the pages of my Bible, examining the words of Jesus for just the right promise. It's important to me in those moments to remember what is true and what He has said He will do. When everything just seems wrong, my deepest desire is to cling to the hope that I know must exist—if only I could find it.

I wonder if the disciples did something similar. When Jesus was killed, shattering their dreams of an overthrown Rome and an earthly victory, did they scan through their memories to find the hope hidden there? Did they rehash every conversation and message? Did they relive every miracle? The funny thing is, Jesus had told them what to expect. He had laid out what would happen on that particular weekend, and yet, it still caught them off guard. In the midst of His death, what they needed more than anything was to simply remember Jesus' own words.

At the Passover meal, often referred to as the last supper, Jesus told His disciples plainly that Judas would betray Him[36] but that He would rise.[37] Earlier that week He had told them that He would be crucified.[38] Well before all of this even, Jesus had divulged His coming death and resurrection no less than three times, plainly including the disciples in the plan set before Him.[39] In His infinite wisdom and kindness, Jesus had given the people closest to Him all the information they needed to weather the coming trial. Unfortunately, when they needed it most, they failed to remember what they had been told.

The truth of Scripture is only valuable to us if we take it to heart. Left on the pages of a dusty book, the hope held within the very Word of God does us no good. In the darkest days of His death, the words of Jesus did not bring the hope they could have imparted, but this was not due to their lack of power. Jesus' words had power then and still have power now. What was the issue then? If Christ's words have power then what went wrong? As always, the problem doesn't lie

---

[36] Matthew 26:21-25
[37] Matthew 26:32
[38] Matthew 26:1-2
[39] Matthew 16:21; 17:22-23; 20:17-19

with our Savior, the problem lies with us. Jesus' words did not bring hope to the hearers because, unlike the Psalmist, they had not "stored up" His words in their hearts.[40] Instead, they had forgotten them—discarding them to fade in the annals of the past.

When Christ was crucified, Mary Magdalene remembered the truth she had been told. While nothing in Scripture seems to suggest that she understood He would rise again so quickly, she at least remembered Who Jesus was and that He was worth following—even in death.

While most of the disciples abandoned Jesus during His crucifixion, Mary stayed.[41] When darkness overcame them, He breathed His last breath, and the curtain was torn. The crowds left but Mary remained.[42] When His body was removed and placed in the tomb, Mary was there.[43] She did not abandon the Lord for one second, but stuck to Him until the end, keeping watch to see that He received a proper burial and even making the effort to ensure His body was anointed. At this point it would be reasonable for her to disregard everything she had believed, abandoning her beliefs and moving on with her life. After all, Jesus had just been killed before her very eyes. Mary didn't do this. In fact, she clung to what she knew and obeyed what had been commanded of her even in the midst of the chaos and confusion of the crucifixion. Mary remembered Who He Was and what He required, taking that

---

[40] Psalm 119:11
[41] John 19:25
[42] Luke 23:44-49
[43] Luke 23:55

dire Saturday to rest as was commanded.[44] "Remember, Mary, remember," we can imagine her thinking. "This is your Rescuer, the One who plunged you out of darkness, brought the blind man sight and caused the dead to live. None of that changes because He is in a tomb." And so, she lived as if nothing had changed because God Himself is unchangeable and no cross or tomb could ever take that away from Mary. She remembered and so she endured.

When God moved in a miraculous way among the nation of Israel, they set up stones as a reminder for future generations of what He had done in that place. In Genesis 28, The Lord met Jacob in a dream. In it, Jacob was shown a stairway to heaven with angels ascending and descending, representing God's work on his behalf. The Lord then promised Jacob that He will be with him, that Jacob's descendants will be numerous, that He would give Jacob the land where he laid, and that all the people of earth would be blessed through his children. To mark the importance of that place and as a reminder of what God promised to do, Jacob set a up stone memorial and renamed that place "Bethel." Years later, Jacob would set up yet another memorial at Bethel, this time to mark what God had already done and to remember what God had promised was to come. Similarly, after God led the Israelites across the Jordan River on dry land, The Lord instructed them to set up stones as a reminder of how He had just provided for them.[45] After God delivered Israel from the Philistines in 1 Samuel 7, Samuel set yet another stone as a memorial of the help God had given them up until that point. Stone after stone placed

---

[44] Luke 23:56
[45] Joshua 4:5-7

as a remembrance of Who God Is and what He had done.

So too we must be women who set up memorials of God working in our lives. Whether it be with tattoos or stones, jewelry or journaling, the things God has done in us and for us must not be forgotten. When the dark Saturdays come, our ability to recall the truth of the gospel is critical to our ability to endure, but not only that, it's critical for others to endure as well. The stones Israel set up were visual reminders for everyone who came after. It wasn't one of those "you had to be there" moments—everyone understood the significance of the stones regardless of whether or not you participated in the event. That meant that whatever you were walking through, you simply had to look at the stones to remember His faithfulness. While we probably don't have rocks placed around our homes and churches for others to see, our stories of the faithfulness of God are still important. When our friends and family members are struggling to trust God, remember for them. When our children are having difficulty believing that the Lord is for them, remind them of the ways God has worked in their family's life. When churches are faced with unprecedented times, point them to the stories in Scripture of His unwavering goodness to His people. Set up stones, figurative or literal, to remember Who He is in your life. Remember for yourself. Remember for your family. Remember for us all.

Go Deeper:

1. What are the ways you have set up stones of remembrance in your life?

2. What stories of God's promises and provision do you have from you or your family's past?

3. Take the time to write out three times God has shown His incredible faithfulness to you. Add to it whenever He answers a prayer or works out a miracle for you. Refer to it whenever you need reminding.

Chapter 7

Present in Christ's Resurrection, We Rejoice

I am a sucker for those home videos of military parents returning home and surprising their children. You know the ones. Oblivious child performing at a recital, receiving an award, or opening up a Christmas gift when suddenly, dad taps them on the shoulder. Usually both parties embrace and tears are shed by everyone witnessing the event. Many big brands have caught on to the trend and used these videos in their ad campaigns. With the added music and emotional catch phrases so characteristic of commercials these days, I can't help but join in, tears streaming down my face as my husband chuckles beside me. After all these years, he has yet to get over the fact that I cry during car commercials. As much as I understand it to be silly, I just can't help it—the beauty of a long-awaited homecoming of a parent will always bring me to tears.

There's something quite special about the love between a parent and a child. Watching my own children with their father is nothing short of magical. My husband was not home often when my oldest was young. Navigating grad school, a full-time job, and internships left us without him most days. Boy, did she feel the absence. I often found her staring out the front window, waiting for her dad to get home.

One particular day when she was just three years old, Alan prepared to leave and found her waiting by the door. She had put her shoes on all by herself and was carrying her toy laptop in her hand. When he inquired as to what she was up to, she made it clear that she was joining him at class that day. "I'm dressed, I have my laptop, I'm all ready!" she exclaimed. Even with abundant embraces and plentiful consolations, she sobbed as she watched him leave without her that morning. He's been home much more consistently for years and even works from home now, but she still finds his presence novel—gasping and hugging him every time he comes downstairs for his hourly coffee refill.

If he so much as runs into town to grab some groceries, this girl will undoubtedly remark that she misses her dad, and when he arrives home will greet him at the door, still jumping into his arms as if she were a toddler. Her intense joy over seeing her father come home is unique among our children. While our others clearly love their father and miss him when he's gone, their reactions are much different. I can't help but think that those several busy years in the beginning of her life have helped shape this part of her. She's the only one old enough to remember the years of his absence, and because she remembers, she can't help but rejoice in his presence.

Mary Magdalene must have felt similarly that dark Sunday morning. Mary was very familiar with being without Jesus—she had spent years trapped in the darkness of oppression—and all of a sudden, she found herself there again. But Mary was different than the crowds. Mary had seen Him enter into her darkness, leaving only light. "Surely He can break through this darkness, as well," we imagine her thinking. "Right?" Early the morning after the Sabbath, while it was still dark, she got up and went to the tomb. Wanting to anoint His body, one final act of love for her Rescuer, Mary was met by Jesus Himself—alive and in the flesh, well and whole. Can you imagine that reunion? This is the reunion above all reunions. This is the surprise of a lifetime—the awaited homecoming that trumps each and every car commercial out there. Jesus had risen from the dead!

I like to imagine Mary laughing and crying as she falls at the feet of her risen Rescuer. At least, I think that's what I would do. You see, Mary had endured, remembered, and obeyed Him even in His absence, and suddenly, there she stood, face to face with the wildest hope she could ever have mustered up. He was alive. Everything had changed for Mary. Again. Would you react differently?

Here's the exciting part—He's still alive. Everything has changed for us too. The resurrection wasn't simply a good day for Mary. It was a good day for us all. In fact, every day since had been good as well. As that stone rolled away, so too did our shame, guilt, and fear, forever giving us reason to rejoice.

The Bible talks a lot about joy and indeed it is one of the key characteristics of believers. Ever since that early Sunday morning in the garden so long ago, we have been a people forever rejoicing. Jesus' death on the cross took away our punishment for our sin and created a way for us to know God, but His resurrection proved His power over the grave, creating a way for us to receive eternal life with our Lord. In light of this overwhelming victory, we have been rejoicing for generations since.

The truth is, we should be known for our ability to rejoice even as we walk through the most trying of situations. When I was a young girl, my grandfather was hit by a drunk driver while walking through a parking lot. He sustained a traumatic brain injury resulting in a nineteen day-long coma and years of after effects. As was usually the case when they were together, my dad and his siblings found themselves laughing and chatting, singing and simply being together in a hospital room. My grandfather's condition and bleak prognosis changed none of that, resulting in hospital staff remarking on how offensive it was that they could be so jovial with their father struggling so. Years later when my own brother was struggling to survive, another hospital staff member would catch me in the bathroom. She explained to me that she had noticed my family over the weeks and just had to know—how could we be so joyful with everything that had happened? As an outsider looking in, our actions did not align with the reality we were experiencing. Rejoicing didn't seem possible in situations like ours.

How can we rejoice when things are arduous, grueling, and overwhelming? The hospital staff at these two hospitals failed to see that our roots were deeply planted in a garden tomb long empty. In one quiet morning, no injury or death could ever again cause us fear. Christ has overcome sin and death, leaving us free to laugh and smile even as we grieve and mourn. With our hearts fully present in a Sunday long passed, our joyful demeanor isn't contrary to the reality around us. In fact, it's just the opposite. When we are reminded of the brokenness in this world through struggle and pain, how much sweeter it is to look back to the peaceful garden and rejoice at what lies ahead. It's a wholly Christian attitude. If death has been over-come, not a thing in this world can rob us of reason to rejoice. Or at least, that's the way it should be.

Too often Christians are indistinguishable from non-Christians in this regard. We look around us and, perhaps rightfully, grow concerned. Brokenness is rampant in this world. The effects of sin seem so evident. Disease and injury leave people we love suffering. Addiction and abuse seem so widespread. We see corruption among our elected officials and begin to question, "Will things ever get better?" Suddenly, our valid concerns turn into worries and dreads. Soon our eyes are no longer fixed on Jesus, but on our fears and disappointments in this world. Rejoicing seems impossible, even in poor taste when everything around us is falling apart. "How can I be joyful when people are suffering?" we ask ourselves. Before we know it, our conversations with believers and nonbelievers alike become political gripe sessions rather than marveling at the faithfulness of God. In switching our focus, we rob ourselves of the ability to experience real joy—and consequently rob everyone around us as well.

Have you ever met someone that "lights up a room?" The kind of person that improves the atmosphere simply by being there? Maybe you have someone in mind or maybe you've been told you are that person. As believers, rooms should be bettered by our presence. Usually, we talk about lighting up a room to describe the loudest, most outgoing, extroverted individual we know. This person often has everyone laughing, keeps parties going well into the night, and knows practically everyone. Maybe you're thinking, "I

could never be that person! I'm too quiet/shy/intro-
verted to light up a room!" I get it. God made us all with
beautiful differences and that means many of us don't
even want to go to a party let alone be the life of it. Fortunately for you, parties aren't required.

Consider Mary, the mother of Jesus. Shortly after
Gabriel visits her to inform her of the role she gets to
play in the birth of the coming Messiah, Mary rushed
to meet her cousin, Elizabeth.[46] During Gabriel's visit,
he had informed Mary that Elizabeth was expecting a
son as well. Mary, most likely wanting to confirm what
she had heard, made haste to visit Elizabeth. Upon
greeting her cousin, Elizabeth has no more than heard
Mary's voice before the Holy Spirit moves upon not
only Elizabeth but her unborn son as well, causing the
baby to leap inside his mother and Elizabeth to cry out
a beautiful blessing upon Mary. Was Mary telling hilar-
ious anecdotes or singing karaoke? Did she bring the
most decadent homemade cake or cookies? No. The
Spirit moved not because of some trait in Mary that
made her likeable, popular, or extra holy, but because
of Who she carried with her. When Mary entered that
home, she brought the Messiah with her, and when the
Messiah enters, nothing remains the same. Elizabeth
and her son, John, recognized the presence of the Lord
and rejoiced, right then and there. We can only assume
the very souls within them were beaming at the coming of the Messiah.

Finding Elizabeth pregnant, and her subsequent reaction to the presence of Jesus, confirmed what Mary
had hoped to be true—that she hadn't simply dreamed
up an elaborate story, that Gabriel had told her the
truth, and that she was indeed carrying the Lord in her

---

[46] Luke 1:39-56

womb. Now Mary is the one who cannot contain her joy, bursting forth in a song of praise to God. Were all her problems solved in that moment or was her life going exactly as planned? Not even a little bit. In fact, as we discussed with Joseph, her life was getting more and more complicated with unexpected difficulty and struggle heading straight for her. She knew that God was leading her into the total unknown and yet we find her rejoicing. Why? Because God had proved Himself true in Gabriel's words to her and was actively fulfilling His promise to redeem His people in the coming of the Messiah. God had spoken. He was working, and that was enough.

A woman present in the resurrection will be a woman who rejoices like Mary. We don't wait until everything is going smoothly to praise the Lord, we rejoice now and always, confident that God is worthy of our praise regardless of our circumstances. After all, a stone was rolled away in a quiet garden all those years ago. How could we not rejoice? As we make rejoicing a daily and soul-level part of ourselves, people will notice.

We may not keep crowds laughing or parties going, but we will bring light with us everywhere we go because we'll bring The Light with us. While we don't carry the Messiah in our wombs like Mary did, we carry Him with us just the same. And just like Mary, our rejoicing spirits will pour out of our hearts and through our mouths and suddenly everyone we meet will feel as though they got to see God a bit more clearly than before. Like my oldest and her dad, we remember what it was like to be out of relationship with God making His presence in our lives that much sweeter. Like Mary, we know what it's like to live in the darkness without Him, but because of the resurrection, no gloomy Saturday, uncertain future, or quiet hospital room could rob us of reason to rejoice—He is risen, and that is enough.

Go Deeper:

1. Do you think that happiness and joy are different? Why or why not?

2. Would you describe yourself as joyful? Would your family? Your friends?

3. List three things you can do to make rejoicing a daily part of your life.

Chapter 8

Present in Christ's Resurrection, We Recount

I sometimes imagine what I would do if my brother gained control of his body again; if his spinal cord was quickly healed, allowing his diaphragm to start contracting and filling his lungs with air, and his arms, legs, fingers and toes to start moving again. After tears and laughter and many long-awaited hugs, each time I let my mind drift there, I always picture myself running through the streets shouting celebrations with arms raised. I imagine myself bursting through doors of friends and family members exclaiming for all to hear, "He's healed! He can move! God did it!" I just don't think I could get that kind of news without telling everyone, without making a scene, without ensuring that not one single person misses out on hearing about the impossible thing God had done.

The truth is, I've already received this kind of news. In fact, thanks to my extraordinary parents, this news was one of the first things I was ever told. There hasn't been a moment in my life that I haven't had life-changing, mountain-moving, nothing-will-ever-be-the-same again news and yet, I have never run through the streets or bounded through doors shouting it out loud. Unfortunately, I tend towards the opposite reaction— keeping it close and personal, waiting for a perfect moment that rarely ever arrives. Sometimes, in my weaker moments, I even act as though this news isn't profound after all—that it's not as important, that it's not for everyone.

Nothing could be more life-altering than the news that Jesus is alive. Victory over death was won in that moment, offering all of humanity hope and healing for eternity, and yet we treat it as though it's a Death Valley "sunny" weather report rather than the top story it is. What's most appalling is that we often are more likely to share our favorite products with our friends than the good news of the gospel. It's not that we don't want to share good things with those around us, it's that we don't want to share The Good Thing. Whether it be a favorite book, podcast, television show, or beauty product, we are quick to share what we love with the people we love—often with the exception of the gospel.

We tell ourselves that it's wise to wait for the right moment or that we don't want to offend anyone when in reality we sidestep the right moments and find offending people acceptable all the time. We proudly tout our political views or opinions on social justice issues while hinting at the truth of the gospel or even worse, leaving it out altogether. We share aggressive memes or tweets with emoji clapping hands when we want our views on current events to be known until our social media stories and timelines are full of anything but Jesus, and then we wonder why the moment is never "right." No, we aren't afraid of offending people, we are afraid of offending people with Jesus, and that's a different thing.

When Mary Magdalene met the risen Savior in the garden that dark morning, she was overwhelmed with joy and hope yet again. Doubtless, she wanted nothing more than to sit in His presence just to be with Him again. But Jesus wouldn't let her. The hope of the resurrection wasn't simply for Mary. It was for everyone. And so, Jesus gave her a job to do immediately, right there beside the tomb. "Go and tell," He said to her. And "Go and tell," He says to us all. Not "Wait until they ask you about your beliefs." Not "Make sure they believe the same thing that you believe before speaking up," or "The resurrection is our special secret," or "You can tell others about Me if they ask, but otherwise keep quiet." No, Jesus said, "Go and tell."

Jesus walked the earth for forty days after the resurrection—before He ascended to The Father.[47] During that time, He imparted to the disciples some of the last things He wanted them to know and remember. Sometime during this time, Jesus brought them to a mountain in Galilee and spoke these words,

> *"Go therefore and make disciples of all nations,*
> *baptizing them in the name of the Father and of the*
> *Son and of the Holy Spirit, teaching them to observe*
> *all that I have commanded you.*
> *And behold, I am with you always, to the end of the*
> *age."*
> Matthew 28:19-20

Often referred to as The Great Commission, this charge was not given to the disciples alone. While yes, the eleven were the only ones present when Jesus spoke these words, the commission to make disciples is given not just to them, but to us as well. As followers of Christ, this is our sacred task. Just like Mary in that garden and the disciples on that mountain, we get to go and tell. Sometimes we think that evangelism,

---

[47] Acts 1:3

spreading the good news of the gospel, is a job left to pastors, missionaries, and other "professional Christians." This is simply not true. Pastors and missionaries are leading the charge, but every man and woman who claims the name of Christ should be following. Not all of us are called to be pastors. All of us are called to go and tell.

We've already discussed the importance of sacrificing whatever is necessary in order to make time to spend in the word. We've observed 2 Timothy 3:16-17 and the many benefits of reading the Bible. We know that the words contained on those pages bring life and hope and joy, and still, we keep them to ourselves. Maybe we share a photo on Instagram with a verse written in calligraphy from time to time. Maybe we tell others we're praying for them. That's enough, right? While sharing Scripture through social media and offering to pray for those around us (and actually doing it) are absolutely wonderful things, without the full truth of the gospel, they aren't enough. In 2 Timothy 4, just after Paul lists the many ways Scripture is beneficial to us, Paul gives Timothy a special charge—preach the word. In fact, it's a message found throughout the entire book of 2 Timothy. In this personal letter to his dear friend, Paul encourages Timothy to remember what he had been taught, to entrust it to faithful men who will continue to teach the gospel, and to be ready to preach the word always. Following 2 Timothy 3:16-17, it's as if Paul is reminding Timothy that since we have such a good gift in Scripture, he should be using it wisely. Luke 12:48 says,

> *Everyone to whom much was given, of him much will be required, and from him to whom they entrusted much, they will demand the more.*

Jesus' words here illustrate the same principle Paul echoed to Timothy. "You've been given a lot. Steward it well."

The charge to Timothy is our charge too. We have been given the very words of God. Are we sharing them with others? In the same way, when we encounter Jesus as Savior and surrender to Him as Lord, our lives should be changed for the better. The world won't suddenly be rose colored. Our problems, and even our earthly consequences for sin, won't magically disappear, but we will have been given a new and exquisite hope, as well as a Comforter, Companion, and Helper. Suddenly, we won't be left under the weight of sin but will be free to live a life for Him. In light of this, how could we not tell everyone we meet what a good God we serve?

I imagine Mary Magdalene running. Having just met the Messiah risen from the dead, dust must have been sticking to her tear-streaked face as her feet kicked up dirt from the road. Maybe she even stumbles in her haste to obey the Christ, but wastes no time getting back on her feet, not even taking the time to dust off her robes as she hurries to the disciples. I can hear her breathing heavily as she throws open the door and yells, "I have seen the Lord!" into a quiet room filled with Jesus' closest friends. Does her haste echo my own?

Another woman, saved from much, shared Mary's excitement to tell the good news. In John 4 we find a "worn out" Jesus resting at a well in Samaria. While there, a woman approach. Alone. In the heat of the day. During their encounter Jesus expresses intimate knowledge of her and her past, ultimately revealing Himself as the Messiah. Reading the account, you can almost see her mind processing this truth before finally leaving the well to tell everyone Who she had just met.

Let's look a bit closer at what is recorded here in John 4. In those days, women would collect water for their families from a well outside the city. To avoid the heat of the day, women would typically go in the morning hours. What brought this woman to the well at noon, then? While we may never know the answer to this question, it isn't unreasonable to surmise that she was there at noon because of her own shame. As Jesus rightly states, she had been married many times and was currently involved with another man that was not her husband. In the culture of the time, that would have been a damning truth, no doubt subjecting her to scrutiny, judgment, and even shunning. Was that the appeal of the well at noon? Nobody around to reject her? Likely she had purposefully chosen to collect water at a time at which she knew the well would be deserted, even if it meant a more difficult job under a scorching sun. To her it was worth it, simply to be alone.

Later in the chapter, this same woman departs the well in such haste that she leaves her water jug behind in order to go into the city and talk with the people that she had just taken such lengths to avoid. What changed? The short answer: everything. Her brief encounter with the Messiah was enough to completely change her objective. Suddenly, her entire reason for coming out to the well in the first place is completely replaced with a new and better purpose. She had met the Messiah, how could she not run and tell?

The Gospels are full of examples of people going and telling. From giving the blind their sight to casting out demons, Jesus' many miracles were witnessed by men and women who couldn't keep quiet. What they saw and experienced was worth sharing to any and everyone around. Consequently, news about Jesus spread quickly and effectively throughout the world, allowing more and more people to come to a saving faith in Christ Jesus. This is the beauty of the gospel—the power to move from death to life. I've seen it. You've seen it. And all we have to do to let other people see it too, is speak.

Mary and the woman at the well understood the importance of what their eyes had just seen. As women present in the resurrection of Christ, we have had our eyes opened to the beauty of the gospel. So too we must run and tell. The good news should be bursting out of us, barely able to be contained. It should be overflowing from our lips and our hands; from the words we type to the photos we share. Everything we do should be driven by our joy in the resurrection and our desire to see every person experience that same hope. Both of these women dropped everything—their shame, their fear, their grief—to give that hope to those around them. Are we doing the same?

Go Deeper:

1. Do you find sharing the hope of the gospel with your family and friends easy? If not, what makes it difficult?

2. Commit to praying for a heart of evangelism for those around you this week. Ask God to give you eyes to see opportunities to talk about Him and the ability to trust Him to give you the words to speak when those opportunities arrive.

3. Take some time to write out a thank you note to whoever shared the gospel with you. Thank them for being brave enough to speak truth to you and share with them how that has impacted your life.

Chapter 9

Present in Christ's Resurrection, We Ready Ourselves

You know those recurring nightmares that find you standing naked in front of a classroom full of people? While I've never had that particular one, I have been plagued by a similar school scenario in my dream life. In mine, I find myself late for class, having slept through my alarm, and unable to get my things together in time. Throughout the entirety of the dream, I am bumbling about, trying to get dressed and to school, only to find that there's an important test being given that I am not only late for, but have yet to study for as well. Even though it's a silly nightmare, I wake up stressed each and every time. It's been over ten years since I've entered a classroom as a student and yet I still have them occasionally. There is just something about being unprepared that has entered my subconscious and made it's home there.

At some level, my insane fear of being found unready serves me well. While I do not anticipate any unexpected math tests being thrown my way in the future, as believers we should be living in a place of expectation. Jesus is returning and we better be found ready.

Several years ago, a group of people had decided that they had "cracked" the case of when Jesus will return. So certain were they of their projected date that they took the time and money to have billboards around the country painted with "Save the Date" type messages of Jesus' imminent return. Maybe you remember them. I can only assume that the intention was to encourage as many people as possible to repent of their sins and turn to the Lord. While I echo the sentiment and agree with the heart, in labeling a specific day the day that Jesus will call the Church home, the creators of the billboards ignored the very word of God. Yes, we should ready, but not because we know which day He is coming. We should be ready for the exact opposite reason—because we don't.

Matthew 24:36 says,

But concerning that day and hour no one knows,
not even the angels of heaven,
nor the Son, but the Father only.

The day being referenced here is not the return of Christ to reign on earth, but the beginning of the day of the Lord and the rapture of the Church.[48] On this day, Jesus will call all the saints on the earth home, leaving only nonbelievers in this world. Can you see the need to be ready? Can you see how our ignorance of the day and hour should urge us forward?

Jesus goes on to liken this day to the days of Noah. Noah had been given specific instructions to ready himself for the flood God had promised to send. If you're familiar with the story, you'll know that these were no small instructions. In Genesis 6:14-21, God says to Noah,

---

[48] Vanlaningham, Michael G. "Matthew." In *The Moody Bible Commentary*, edited by Michael Rydelnik and Michael Vanlaningham, 1533. Chicago: Moody Publishers, 2014.

"Make yourself an ark of gopher wood. Make rooms in the ark, and cover it inside and out with pitch. This is how you are to make it: the length of the ark 300 cubits, its breadth 50 cubits, and its height 30 cubits. Make a roof for the ark, and finish it to a cubit above, and set the door of the ark in its side. Make it with lower, second, and third decks. For behold, I will bring a flood of waters upon the earth to destroy all flesh in which is the breath of life under heaven. Everything that is on the earth shall die. But I will establish my covenant with you, and you shall come into the ark, you, your sons, your wife, and your sons' wives with you. And of every living thing of all flesh, you shall bring two of every sort into the ark to keep them alive with you. They shall be male and female. Of the birds according to their kinds, and of the animals according to their kinds, of every creeping thing of the ground, according to its kind, two of every sort shall come in to you to keep them alive. Also take with you every sort of food that is eaten, and store it up. It shall serve as food for you and for them."

In order for Noah and his family to survive, he was required to build an elaborate ark and fill it will every kind of animal on the earth and every kind of food. Can you imagine being given instructions like these? I can only imagine how daunting this must have felt to Noah. I often feel overwhelmed after reading the directions for a new board game—instructions like these might very well send me into a panic attack!

What an extraordinary task was set before him! This huge undertaking is estimated to have taken him as many as seventy-five years. Seventy-five years! During that time, we are only told God spoke to him once more. Seven days before the flood, God speaks again, telling Noah to enter the ark. In the time between Noah given his instructions and the rains beginning, do you think he ever wondered if the flood would really come? Do you think Noah ever questioned the importance of building such a monstrous boat in the decades before it was needed? As Genesis tells us, the world was increasingly wicked at this point, so much so that the Bible says "every intention of the thoughts of man's heart was only evil continuously."[49] Matthew 24:38-39 says that the people around Noah continued to live their lives normally while Noah prepared, eating, drinking, and all around making merry. Do you think that Noah ever considered abandoning his task and joining in on the fun? It's altogether reasonable to assume that occasionally Noah wondered if it was all worth it. But regardless of the wondering, he persevered and pressed forward. His dedication paid off. Unlike the entirety of the world besides his family, when the flood waters came, he was prepared. He was ready. He survived.

Like Noah, we have been given instructions for how to survive the coming wrath of God. While those instructions don't require us to build a boat and that wrath will not include a worldwide flood, the instructions are worth heeding all the same. What are our instructions, then? How will we escape the wrath of God? The Bible makes it clear that there is only one way and it can be found in perhaps it's most famous verse, a verse many of us learned with our very first words—John 3:16.

---

[49] Genesis 6:5

For God so loved the world, that he gave his only Son, that whoever believes in him should not perish but have eternal life.

Believe. Those are our instructions. No ark. No animals. No food. Just believe and we will not perish. When we talk about freedom in Christ, this is it. This is the moment. The Old Testament believers were tied to lists and lists of rules they had to follow in order to be right before God—to be found ready. In Christ, we simply have to believe.

In Luke 12:35-37, Jesus says,

"Stay dressed for action and keep your lamps burning, and be like men who are waiting for their master to come home from the wedding feast, so that they may open the door to him at once when he comes and knocks. Blessed are those servants whom the master finds awake when he comes."

Then in verse 40, He says,

"You also must be ready, for the Son of Man is coming at an hour you do not expect."

To ready ourselves for whatever God has today and for whenever God brings The Day of The Lord, we simply have to believe, and keep believing. To be dressed for action is to clothe ourselves with the armor of God daily. To keep our lamps burning is to let the Word of God dwell richly in us. To be found awake is to be actively seeking God in Scripture and prayer; and not only seeking, but responding. When Christ finds His people awake, blessed they will be, indeed.

When Jesus rose from the dead all those years ago, Mary Magdalene was ready. She had followed Jesus throughout His life and death and was unwilling to abandon her beliefs, even if it would have benefited her in the short term. Because of her devotion to Christ, she was the first person to see the risen Lord. What an honor. What an experience.

As a teenager, my parents drove a Chevy truck with a distinctive sound. Even with music on, friends over, or movies blaring, both my brother and I could recognize the sound of it approaching from blocks away. This was particularly helpful, allowing us time to tidy up and act like we had been doing something productive (teenagers, am I right?).

That short notice made all the difference in how we were found when our parents walked through the doors, and you can bet we took advantage of it. We won't be given that same privilege as believers, so we must live our lives differently each and every day. Women present in the resurrection of Christ will ready ourselves daily, ensuring that Christ not return and find us asleep or slacking off. Unlike Noah, we won't be given a week's notice allowing us to get our affairs in order. Unlike my teenage self, there will be no sound of the parents coming up the street to permit us time to tidy and look busy. We are either ready, or we aren't. We believe or we don't; either way, we'll be held accountable. He's coming back. He's calling us home. We don't know how or when or where, but He's promised it will happen. In our lifetime or another, He will return. Someday, we will stand before God and give an account for our actions. Only the blood of Christ will cover our sins. Only belief in Him readies us for that day.

The apostle Paul warns us to "not grow weary of doing good."[50] It's a trap we so easily fall into. After all, we're only people. I imagine Noah was tempted to fall into this same trap time and time again. I imagine there were many things he would rather have been doing than building a giant boat and preparing to gather and feed thousands of animals. Doubtless he was mocked and judged by the people around him.

Maybe he considered calling it quits and going on to live his life like everyone else around him. Could you blame him? There were seventy-five years between the promise of the flood and the fulfillment of that promise. That's a long time to believe and keep believing. That's a long time to stay alert. So too, we can grow weary of believing. We can get tired of following Christ. Sometimes it seems like we've been waiting for God for literal decades—holding out for that miracle, looking for that breakthrough, or pleading for things to just get easier. I've been there. I'm sure you have too.

Paul's instructions are for those seasons. Don't grow weary. Some of us might be tempted to put off getting right with God until we've lived our lives and had our fun. Can you imagine Noah doing that? Just deciding he'd get ready for the flood when it got a little closer? God gave him only seven days' notice—not nearly enough time to save himself, let alone his family and all the animals on earth. And that's just the point. We don't have enough time, enough skill, enough goodness to save ourselves. We don't know when we will die. We don't know when Christ will return. All we know is we have this day, this hour, this minute to choose to follow Christ in His resurrection, readying

---

[50] Galatians 6:9

ourselves for whatever may come. Don't grow weary of believing. Don't grow weary of following Jesus. Don't grow weary and fall asleep. Jesus is real. He's risen. And He's coming back. Best be found ready.

Go Deeper:

1. Were Christ to return today, would you be ready? If not, what do you need to do to ensure you are right before God?

2. Read the Parable of The Ten Virgins in Matthew 25. Ask God to give you a watchful countenance—continually looking for The Lord.

3. Read the Parable of The Talents, also in Matthew 25. Spend some time listing out the resources you have available to you, including your gifts, talents, and abilities. Which two can you better use this week to advance the Kingdom of God and bring Him glory?

Conclusion

Were you to sit with Mary Magdalene today, I doubt that she would consider herself a worthy example to believing women. While her story in Scripture is short and hardly remarkable, her steady faithfulness is one we can all seek to exemplify. Mary, like us, was rescued from much. She experienced beautiful disruption and sacrificed daily for the sake of the gospel. She chose to follow her Rescuer, leading others along as she went. She endured incredible trials and difficult unknowns, all while seeking after The Messiah. She obeyed even in her confusion and fear, and intentionally chose to remember the teachings of Christ. She rejoiced in His resurrection and recounted the beauty of that remarkable morning, and she ensured she was ready to do the work that He required, whatever that might be. She was neither royal nor distinguished, extraordinarily talented or astonishingly clever, but her example has endured to this day. Mary was faithful with little and faithful with much. So too, we can be faithful with whatever God gives.

What does devotion to Christ look like in a woman? It's not something we can purchase or wear. You can't spot it in a crowd. There is no monthly subscription box for everything required. Devotion is a choice—a million little choices daily. Choices, that when tallied, add up to a life of devotion to our King. Mary made them. So, can you.

As women present in Christ's life, we will welcome disruption, no matter how scary. We will sacrifice ourselves for the first thing in order to sacrifice for the second. We will follow the women ahead of us so we can lead the women behind. In Christ's death, we will endure trial and suffering and rejection all for the glory of God. We will choose a life of obedience even when it's not popular—even when it costs us something. We will remember the truth of Scripture and His working in our lives time and time again. His resurrection will call us to rejoice, even if everything around us seems to be falling apart, for Christ has overcome sin and death. We will recount the hope that we have and the miracles that He's worked and we will ready ourselves daily, for this is the will of the Lord. And through all of this, as we walk in His life, in His death, and His resurrection, we will get to experience the gift of His presence, the power of His grace, and the hope of His coming. If Mary could do it, so can we. Praise Him.

ABOUT
KHARIS PUBLISHING

KHARIS PUBLISHING is an independent, traditional publishing house with a core mission to publish impactful books, and channel proceeds into establishing mini-libraries or resource centers for orphanages in developing countries, so these kids will learn to read, dream, and grow. Every time you purchase a book from Kharis Publishing or partner as an author, you are helping give these kids an amazing opportunity to read, dream, and grow. Kharis Publishing is an imprint of Kharis Media LLC. Learn more at https://www.kharispublishing.com.

CPSIA information can be obtained
at www.ICGtesting.com
Printed in the USA
FSHW022147310121
78202FS